The Process of Buddhist-Christian Dialogue

The Process of Buddhist-Christian Dialogue

PAUL O. INGRAM

CASCADE *Books* · Eugene, Oregon

THE PROCESS OF BUDDHIST-CHRISTIAN DIALOGUE

Cascade Books
A Division of Wipf and Stock Publishers
199 W. 8th Ave., Suite 3
Eugene, OR 97401

www.wipfandstock.com

ISBN 13: 978-1-60608-554-7

Cataloging-in-Publication data:

Ingram, Paul O., 1939-

The process of Buddhist-Christian dialogue / Paul O. Ingram.

ISBN 13: 978-1-60608-554-7

xii + 150 p. ; 23 cm. —Includes bibliographic references.

1. Christianity and other religions—Buddhism. 2. Buddhism—Relations—Christianity. I. Title.

BQ 7436 I54 2009

Manufactured in the U.S.A.

Contents

List of Figures

Preface

Much has been written about process Buddhist-Christian dialogue. In all probability much more will be written. But thus far no author has published a book about contemporary Buddhist-Christian dialogue from the perspective of Whiteheadian process thought, although process philosophers and theologians have written numerous essays on the topic. Nor have many writers sought to expand the current Buddhist-Christian dialogue into a "trilogue" by means of bringing the natural sciences into the discussion as a "third partner," which was the topic of my *Buddhist-Christian Dialogue in an Age of Science*. My thesis in *The Process of Buddhist-Christian Dialogue* is that Buddhist-Christian dialogue in all three of its forms—conceptual, social engagement, and interior—are interdependent processes, the nature of which is helpfully characterized through the categories of Whiteheadian process thought. Process thought asserts that process is fundamental to not only human experience, but to the structure of reality, "the way things and events really are." I have appropriated some of the categories of Whitehead's process metaphysics throughout the specific chapters in this book as a means of analyzing contemporary Buddhist-Christian dialogue and this dialogue's encounter with the natural sciences. Accordingly, references to the Whiteheadian foundations of my understanding of the process of Buddhist-Christian dialogue support each chapter of this book.

Chapter 1, "That We May Know Each Other," argues that what philosopher John Hick called "the pluralist hypothesis," when stripped of its Kantian assumptions and reinterpreted in the categories of Whitehead's understanding of God, offers the most coherent framework from which to interpret our post-modern experience of religious pluralism. As a means of demonstrating this thesis I have also appropriated philosopher of science Imre Lakotos' account of the methodology of scientific research programs. The goal of this chapter is to clarify the foundational assumptions underlying my particular account of contemporary Buddhist-Christian dialogue.

Chapters 2–5 are historical in nature because in these chapters I offer a descriptive summary of the three interdependent forms of Buddhist-Christian dialogue that have emerged to this date. My intention is to demonstrate the specific structures of process Buddhist-Christian dialogue. Chapter 2, "The Structure of Buddhist-Christian Conceptual Dialogue," summarizes important Buddhist and Christian writers who have emphasized this form of dialogue in their conversations. The focus of conceptual dialogue is doctrinal, theological, and philosophical because it focuses on a religious community's collective self-understanding and worldview. In conceptual dialogue, Buddhists and Christians compare and contrast theological and philosophical formulations on such questions as ultimate reality, human nature, suffering and evil, the role of the historical Jesus in Christian faith and practice, the role of the Buddha in Buddhist teaching and practice, and what Buddhists and Christians might learn and appropriate from one another.

The title of chapter 3 is "Conceptual Dialogue with the Natural Sciences." Its thesis is that including the natural sciences into conceptual, socially engaged, and interior Buddhist-Christian dialogue as a third partner will engender new processes of creative transformation in both Buddhist and Christian traditions. "Buddhist-Christian Socially Engaged Dialogue" is the topic of chapter 4. Buddhist-Christian conceptual dialogue has generated deep interest in the relevance of dialogue for issues of social, environmental, economic, and gender justice. Since these issues are systemic, global, interconnected, and interdependent, they are neither religion-specific nor cultural-specific. Accordingly, this chapter is a description of how Buddhists and Christians have mutually apprehended common experiences and resources for working together to help human beings liberate themselves and nature from the global forces of systemic oppression.

Chapter 5, "Buddhist-Christian Interior Dialogue," is about how in the human struggle for liberation Buddhist and Christians share an experiential "common ground" that enables them to hear one another and be mutually transformed in the process. The emphasis of this chapter is Buddhist and Christian practice traditions—meditation and centering prayer traditions. Finally in chapter 6, "Creative Transformation at the Boundaries," I bring Buddhist-Christian dialogue and dialogue with the natural sciences into confrontation with "boundary questions" that are generated by Buddhism's and Christianity's structuring worldviews in relation to scientific boundary questions. It is in this chapter that I discuss the issues of transcendence in Christianity, Buddhism, and the natural sciences as a means of establishing a foundation for an ongoing process of Buddhist-Christian-science trilogue that is at present only beginning to occur.

At this juncture, it would be helpful to clarify meaning of "dialogue" as I understand this term before proceeding further. For most persons dialogue is a process, to appropriate the words of John S. Dunn, of "passing over and returning."[1] In interreligious dialogue we pass over into the lives of persons whose religious traditions are different than our own, appropriate what we can into our own lives, identify what cannot be appropriated, and return to our own faith community. In the process, our intellects are stretched and our imaginations deepened, or, in the language of process theology, "creatively transformed." And since the purpose of interreligious dialogue is most often the renewal of one's own faith commitments and faith community—otherwise why engage in dialogue at all?—at least four conditions must be met before such creative transformation can occur.

First, no ulterior motives of any sort should be the incentive for engaging in dialogue. Approaching another religious standpoint with hidden agendas provides only limited results, usually more negative than positive. For example, engaging in dialogue with a Buddhist merely for the purpose of comparing Buddhist doctrine and practice with Christian doctrine and practice in order to evangelize Buddhists undermines the integrity of Christian and Buddhist tradition. Engaging in dialogue in order to convert persons to one's own particular faith tradition is a monologue, not a dialogue. Interreligious dialogue is not missionology.

Second, dialogical engagement with persons dwelling in faith communities other than our own enriches our faith and practice, as well as the faith and practices of our dialogical partner. Nothing valuable can emerge from interreligious dialogue unless our perspectives are genuinely challenged, tested, and stretched by the faith and practice of our dialogical partner. Approaching other religious persons merely as advocates of our own faith commitments and community confuses dialogue with monologue and engenders religious imperialism.

Third, interreligious dialogue demands accurate, critical, and articulate understanding of our own faith traditions as well as the traditions of our dialogical partner. The process of creative transformation through dialogue rests upon being engaged by the truth claims of our own religious traditions

1. Dunn, *The Way of All the Earth*, iv.

well as the truth claims of our dialogical partners. For without a point of view critically held, dialogue with others is transformed into a mere sharing of ideas—we share our views and our partners share theirs, and nothing of value is achieved. Individuals who have heard the lyrics and music of their own faith communities are more likely to hear and understand the music and lyrics of a tradition other than their own. It's a bit like being in love. As our own experiences of giving and receiving love allows us to apprehend and appreciate love experienced by other human beings, so our own religious experiences, critically understood, allow us to enter into the ideas and experiences of persons participating in religious traditions other than our own.

Finally, dialogue is a quest for truth where "truth" is understood as relational in structure. Truth can have no confessional boundaries in a universe governed by general and special relativity. Interreligious dialogue is meaningful as it grows out of our common humanity as persons whose sense of what it means to be human expresses itself through different, yet valid and real, encounters with the Sacred, however the Sacred is named. This does not imply that all truth claims have equal truth-value. In dialogue we become aware not only of similarities, but differences between ourselves and other persons. For this reason alone, dialogue is not for the intellectually or spiritually fainthearted. We are never the same person after a dialogue as we were before we entered into dialogue. The truths we believe, the assumptions we have, the experiences we have undergone, will be challenged, after which we return "home" to our own faith traditions with fewer exclusivist assumptions about religious standpoints other than our own. But even here, there are no guarantees. Some persons may not return to their traditions after passing over into another. The contemporary history of Buddhist-Christian dialogue is replete with Christians who have passed over into Buddhism and made Buddhism their spiritual home. Buddhists who have dialogically passed over into Christian traditions have sometimes remained in the Christian community. Some Buddhists and Christians have acquired a dual religious identity as "Buddhist-Christian" or "Christian-Buddhist." Whether one remains in one's own community or enters another community or acquires a multiple religious identity through the practice of interreligious dialogue, the process of creative transformation through dialogue has been at work.

An author's work never gets into print without the assistance of many people. Among the persons to which I wish to offer my thanks are Fr. Francis Tiso, editor emeritus of *Buddhist-Christian Studies*, for permission to include an essay published in this journal in 2004 as the first chapter of *The Process of*

Buddhist-Christian Dialogue. I am also grateful to the editors of the University of Hawaii Press and the publisher of *Buddhist-Christian Studies* for allowing me to incorporate my 2004 essay in this volume. K. C. Hanson, the editor in chief of Wipf and Stock Publishers and Cascade Books, served as editor of this volume. I also wish to express my gratitude to Kristen Bareman, who typeset the book. The more I have worked with Wipf and Stock Publishers over the years, the more I am amazed at just how professional its staff is.

Finally, I wish to dedicate this book to my daughter and her husband, Gail Ingram Kinner and David Charles Kinner, and their young son, David Christian, and my son, Robert William Ingram. The grace of their lives continually flows into my wife's and my lives in ways that often stuns us to silence. Finally, my wife, Regina Inslee Ingram, has always supported my work and is the center of my life around which everything I hold dear revolves. She is the glue that holds my family together.

Paul O. Ingram
Mukilteo, Washington
April 22, 2009

1

That We May Know Each Other[1]

When an African-American Muslim named Siraj Wahaj served as the
first Muslim "Chaplain of the Day" in the Unites States House of
Representatives on June 25, 1991, he offered the following prayer, the first
Muslim prayer in the in the history of the House of Representatives:

> In the name of God, Most Gracious, Most Merciful. Praise belongs
> to Thee alone; O God, Lord and Creator of all the worlds. Praise
> belongs to Thee Who shaped us and colored us in the wombs of
> our mothers; colored us black and white, brown, red, and yellow.
> Praise belongs to Thee who created us from males and females and
> made us into nations and tribes that we may know each other.[2]

Siraj Wahaj's prayer is a direct reference to one of the most cited verses
of the Qur'an: "Do you not know, O people, that I have made you into
tribes and nations that you may know each other?" Of course, "knowing
each other" is an important goal in the practice of interreligious dialogue,
but Muslims often move on to cite further Qur'anic advice about religious
pluralism: "If God had so willed, He Would have made you a single people,"
the verse reads, "But His plan is to test you in what He hath given you; so
strive as in a race in all virtues."[3] According to Siraj Wahaj and many like-
minded American Muslims, Islam and pluralism go hand in hand and respect

1. This chapter is an essay originally published in *Buddhist-Christian Studies*. I wish to
express my thanks to Fr. Francis Tiso, editor emeritus of *Buddhist-Christian Studies*, and
the publisher of this journal, the University of Hawaii Press, for permission to include
this essay in this book.

2. *American Muslim Council Report* (Summer 1991), cited in Eck, *A New Religious
America*, 32.

3. Surah 5.51, A. Yasuf Ali, trans.

1

for the dignity for each person, no matter what religious or secular label he or she wears, rests on Islamic foundations. Of course, this interpretation of the Qur'an is rejected by radical communities within the House of Islam as well as by fundamentalist communities within Christian, Buddhist, Hindu, and Jewish tradition. Nor are the foundations of pluralism only found in the Qur'an. Buddhist, Jewish, Hindu, Christian, and aboriginal traditions support religious pluralism as well.

This chapter's thesis is that what John Hick first posited as the "pluralist hypothesis" offers us the most coherent theoretical framework—minus Hick's Kantian epistemology—from which to interpret contemporary post-modern experience of religious diversity. Furthermore, I shall argue that the pluralist hypothesis constitutes a coherent history of religions research program from which to investigate and interpret the facts of religious diversity.[4] In order to demonstrate the adequacy of my thesis and argument, I shall appropriate the philosopher of science Imre Lakatos' account of the methodology and structure of scientific research programs, guided by Nancy Murphy's application of Lakatos' work in the construction of theological research programs. But first, some preliminary clarifications about what I mean by "religious pluralism" and "religious diversity."[5]

THE STRUCTURE OF THE EXPERIENCE OF
RELIGIOUS PLURALISM

In a recent book on the lives of four Catholic writers—Dorothy Day, Thomas Merton, Flannery O'Connor, and Walker Percy—Paul Elie provides one of the most accurate descriptions of the structure of post-modern experience of religious diversity in English print.

> We are all skeptics now, believer and unbeliever alike. There is no one faith, evident at all times and places. Every religion is one among many. The clear lines of orthodoxy are made crooked by our experience, and are complicated by our lives. Believer and unbeliever are in the same predicament, thrown back onto ourselves in complex circumstances, looking for a sign. As ever, religious

4. While I accept most of Hick's arguments in support of the pluralist hypothesis, I do not assume the Kantian epistemological foundations of Hick's account of religious pluralism. See Hick, *An Interpretation of Religion*, chapter 14. What follows in this chapter will be written from the perspective of one convinced of the truth of Whiteheadian process metaphysics and epistemology.

5. See Eck's description of religious pluralism in *A New Religious America*, 70–77.

belief makes its claim somewhere between revelation and projection, between holiness and human frailty, but the problem of proof, indeed the burden of belief, for so long upheld by society, is now back on the believer, where it should be.[6]

Assuming that Elie's description is an accurate one, certain implications follow that will serve as working assumptions for the remainder of this book.

- "Pluralism" is not just another name for "diversity." Diversity names the fact of the existence of differing religious traditions among human beings. Pluralism goes beyond mere diversity to active engagement with religious plurality. Religious diversity is an observable fact all over the world, but perhaps most observable in America. But without engagement with one another, the mere facts of the existence of neighboring churches, temples, and mosques are just salad bowl examples of diversity. We can study diversity, celebrate it, or complain about it, but diversity alone is not pluralism. Pluralism is not an empirical fact, as religious diversity is an empirical fact. Pluralism is an attitude, a theological orientation, a theoretical construct that seeks to coherently interpret and understand the data of religious diversity.

- Pluralism as a theoretical construct is not an ideology, nor a Western neo-liberal scheme, nor a debilitating form of relativism.[7] Pluralism is best understood as a dynamic process through which we dialogically engage with one another through our very deepest differences. Throughout this book I shall appropriate the metaphysics of Whiteheadian process philosophy as a means of conceptualizing pluralism as a dynamic process of creative transformation.

- Pluralism as a theoretical construct is not mere tolerance of "the other," but is an active attempt to understand the other. Although tolerance is a step forward from intolerance, it does not require neighbors to know one another. Tolerance can create a climate of restraint, but not understanding. Tolerance does little to overcome stereotypes and fears that in

6. Elie, *The Life You Save May Be Your Own*, 472.

7. See the collection of essays edited by D'Costa, *Christian Uniqueness Reconsidered*. Each contributor to this volume, in varying ways, argues that pluralist theologies of religions are in fact forms of debilitating relativism, a Western form of intellectual imperialism that reduces the diversity of the world's religious traditions to a particular metaphysic, thereby committing what Whitehead called the "fallacy of misplaced concreteness," and therefore are fundamentally ahistorical.

fact govern the lives of many religious persons when they encounter the religious "other." Pluralism is a theological-philosophical move beyond tolerance based on exclusivist and inclusivist theologies of religions toward a constructive understanding of what to make of the empirical facts of religious diversity.[8]

- Pluralism as a theoretical construct is not debilitating relativism. It does not displace or eliminate deep religious or secular commitments. Pluralism is the encounter of commitments. Many critics of pluralism persist in linking pluralism with a kind of valueless relativism, in which all perspectives are equally compelling and, as a result, equally uncompelling. Pluralism, they contend, undermines commitment to one's own particular faith with its own particular language by watering down differences in the interests of universality. I consider this view a distortion of the process of pluralism because pluralism is engagement with, not abdication of, differences and particularities. While encountering people of other faiths may lead to less myopic views of one's own faith, pluralism is not premised on a reductive relativism. The focus of pluralism is on significant engagement with real differences.

- The language of pluralism is dialogue—vigorous engagement, even argument, is essential to a democratic society. Dialogue is vital to the health of a religious faith so that we appropriate our faith not by habit or heritage alone, but by making it our own within the context of conversation with people of other faiths. Dialogue is aimed not at achieving mere agreement, but at achieving relationship. Dialogue as the language of pluralism is the language of engagement, involvement, and participation.

- As a theoretical construct, pluralism is never a complete process, but the ongoing work of each generation.

IMRE LAKATOS ON SCIENTIFIC RESEARCH PROGRAMS

Imre Lakatos's most influential essay is titled "Falsification and the Methodology of Scientific Research Programs." According to Nancy Murphy, Lakatos describes the actual practice of science in terms of competing research paradigms, rather than a historical series of complex competing paradigms, as it

8. See my books, *Wrestling with the Ox*, chap. 2; and *The Modern Buddhist-Christian Dialogue*, chap. 2, for my critique of contemporary exclusive and inclusive theologies of religions.

was for Thomas Kuhn.[9] Lakatos described some of these research programs as "progressive" and others as "degenerating." A degenerating research program is one whose core theory is "saved by ad hoc modifications" that form a protective belt—"mere face-saving devises, or linguistic tricks"—meant to protect the core theory from criticism. As Murphy points out, it is difficult to know what "ad hoc modifications" mean, since it is always difficult to propose criteria for determining what these non-scientific face-saving modifications are.[10]

Lakatos was clear, however, on the conditions necessary for a progressive scientific research program. First, each new version of the theory—what he called its core theory and its hypothesis—preserves the unrefuted content of its predecessor, for example as Einstein's general and special theories of relativity preserved the unrefuted content of Newtonian physics. The function of the core theory is to unify the program by providing a general view of the nature of the entities being investigated. Second, a "protective belt of hypotheses," which function as lower-level theories that support the core theory, surrounds the theoretical core. Also included here are theories of instrumentation and statements of initial conditions. Third, there must be empirical data that support both the core theory and the hypothesis. When the first and second conditions are met, a scientific theory is said to be theoretically progressive. When all three conditions are met the research program is also empirically progressive.[11]

In the actual practice of the natural sciences deductive reason based on hypotheses makes explanation and confirmation symmetrical. That is, the hypotheses nearest the data being researched explain the data, and higher-level hypotheses explain lower-level theories, while the core theory is the ultimate principle for all data. For this reason, Lakatos described the auxiliary hypothesis as a "protective belt," since potentially falsifying data are accounted for by making changes at the level of the auxiliary hypotheses rather than in the core theory, which he called the "hard core" because it cannot be abandoned without abandoning the entire research program, as illustrated in figure 1.1 below. Thus a progressive research program is fundamentally a temporal series of networks of theory, along with supporting data, in which the core theory stays the same but the auxiliary hypotheses change over time to account for new data and the data's relation to the research program's "hard core."

9. Murphy, *Theology in the Age of Scientific Reasoning*, 58–61; see Kuhn, *The Structure of Scientific Revolutions*.

10. Murphy, *Theology in the Age of Scientific Reasoning*, 59.

11. Ibid., 59–60; see also Murphy and Ellis, *On the Moral Nature of the Universe*, 11–13.

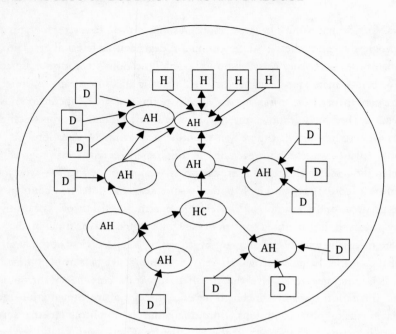

Figure 1.1: Structure of a Scientific Research Program

A progressively mature scientific research program also involves what Lakatos called a "positive heuristic," which is a plan for systematic development of the program to take account of broad arrays of new data. This reflects the recognition of the role of models in contemporary philosophy of science. Scientists employ a wide variety of models, for example the double helix model of DNA or other mathematical and physical models of various sorts. The function of a positive heuristic is to envision the development of a series of increasingly accurate models of the processes and entities under scientific investigation. For example, the hard core of Isaac Newton's research program consisted of his three laws of motion and the law of gravitation as influence at a distance. The auxiliary hypotheses included initial conditions and applications of the three laws of motion and gravity to specific problems. The positive heuristic included working out increasingly sophisticated explanations for the orbits of planets: first calculations for a one-planet system with the sun as a point-mass, then solutions for more planets.

Lakatos's description of the structure of scientific research programs places high value on coherence, yet is open to two criticisms: (1) the arguments that justify conclusions are circular, since it is a matter of each part of the theory fitting into the other parts, and (2) it is difficult to judge between two competing and equally coherent research programs, which seems to imply a debilitating relativism. In reply to this objection, Lakatos proposed that a progressive research program is one in which a new hypothesis accounts for the anomaly that led to its inclusion in the program, but also allows for the prediction and corroboration of novel facts, meaning facts not to be expected in light of the previous version of the research program. Thus a progressive program's factual foundations increase over time, while a degenerating program's empirical content does not increase to keep pace with the increasing proliferation of empirical data.[12] In other words, the justifications for scientific truth grounded in a particular scientific research program are always pragmatic and historical.

Murphy argues that the scientific methodology described by Lakatos can be applied directly to theology as an academic discipline.[13] As one of several examples, she cites Wolfhart Pannenberg's theology, where the hard core is his claim that the God of Jesus is the all-determining reality. This is Pannenberg's central theory that guides the development of his entire theological program. Like a scientific research program, the positive heuristic of any systematic theology like's Pannenberg's is to engender theories ("auxiliary hypotheses") that meet the following conditions: (1) they are faithful to authoritative pronouncements within particular faith communities; (2) they elaborate or spell out the content of the hard core in a way that (3) relates a community's doctrines to available data (sacred texts, the authoritative teaching of a community evolving over time, the experiences of participants in a community). In Pannenberg's example, the hard core—his insistence on God's relation to all that has been, is, or will be—requires that "data" include not only biblical texts, but facts and theories from all areas of knowledge, including the natural sciences interpreted through the hard core of his research program.

PLURALISM AS A THEOLOGICAL RESEARCH PROGRAM

The simple fact of religious diversity, Hick writes, in itself raises no serious theological issues. "It is only when we add what can be called "the basic

---

12. For a detailed discussion of "novel facts," see Murphy, "Another Look at Novel Facts."

13. See Murphy, *Theology in the Age of Scientific Reasoning*, chap. 6, for examples of particular theological research programs as well as an outline of her particular research program.

religious conviction that a problem is generated."[14] By "basic religious conviction," Hick means the conviction that our religious beliefs, practices, and experiences are not illusions because they refer to a transcendent reality, which he calls "the Real." Whether such convictions are justifiable is one of the central issues of philosophy of religion. But Hick's point is that all religious persons claim that their beliefs and practices bear ontological reference to a transcendent reality, named and experienced differently within the contexts of humanity's various religious traditions. This constitutes the hard core of Hick pluralist hypothesis and my notion of pluralism as a research program.

Most often, according to Hick, the basic religious conviction carries an additional claim: one's particular religious tradition is the most valid response to "the Real" because it bears an ontological correspondence to "the Real" missing from religious traditions other than one's own. But can such claims—which most participants in all religious traditions assert in their distinctive ways—ever be validated? Hick thinks they cannot since the wider religious life of humanity occurs within the limits imposed by historical and cultural experience. That is, we can only experience and judge truth claims from the particular historical and cultural contexts through which experiences are lived and judgments are made. Thus Hick's conclusion: no one can know the Sacred "as such," but only as mediated through the filters of history, tradition, and culture.

It is this philosophical conclusion, Kantian in its epistemological assumptions, that leads Hick to posit the pluralistic hypothesis. If (1) the basic assumption of humanity's religious traditions is the existence of an absolutely transcendent and real reality (the hard core), then (2) all of humanity's religious traditions should be understood as auxiliary hypotheses, meaning "different ways of experiencing, conceiving, and living in relation to an ultimate divine reality which transcends all our visions of it."[15] Accordingly, different forms of religious experience that engender different teachings, practices, and images are not necessarily contradictory or competitive in the sense that the truth of one entails the falsehood of the other. In Hick's understanding, all religious traditions reflect encounters with "the Real" within the context of their particular historical and cultural perspectives.

Hick's pluralist hypothesis has been sharply, and perhaps unjustly, criticized for establishing the truth of multiple religious traditions by reducing them to a single common element that assets that the religions of the world

14. Hick, *God Has Many Names*, 88.

15. Hick, *An Interpretation of Religion*, 237.

are really identical at their cores. In point of fact, this is not Hick's claim. He understands perfectly well the diversity of truth claims in the world's religions. A Kantian epistemology might allow one to take such an ahistorical position. But Kantian as he is, Hick does not draw this conclusion. The hard core of his theory is that the religious traditions of humanity embody historical experience with an "ultimate reality," which he calls "The Real." His auxiliary hypotheses do not reduce the historical complexity of the world's religions to a single common element.

My contention is that one can meet objections to the pluralist hypothesis by (1) appropriating Lakatos' model of how scientific research programs actually function, and (2) reformulating the pluralist hypothesis in terms of Whiteheadian process thought. The hard core of my research program agrees with Hick: all religious traditions reflect culturally and historically limited experiences of a reality that transcends them all, and they all seek to describe this reality in their own terms according to their own traditions. But this reality is incredibly complex and what the religious traditions of the world teach about this reality are not identical; they *do not* say the same things even though they are referencing the same Sacred reality. Instead, each particular religious tradition expresses truths intended to be universal, but not the full truth. That is, the specific religions of the world constitute a series of auxiliary hypotheses intended as true accounts of reality, meaning the way things really are as opposed to the way we want things to be, even though the teachings and practices of the world's religions are often similar, often different, sometimes contradictory, and occasionally complementary in their differences. A corollary of this reformulation is that *some* teachings and practices in all the world's religions *do* bear ontological correspondence to the reality to which they refer.

In this reformulation, the world's religious traditions potentially express truth claims that either complement or contradict each other. This assumes that different religious traditions address aspects of the human condition relative to their particular culture and history, so that attention must be paid to these differences. Thus, for example, Buddhist concepts of Awakening and Christian concepts of salvation are different and express different religious experiences of the Sacred. But by understanding the differences and raising questions in dialogue, Buddhists and Christians can enrich their own understanding of reality.

The primary mode of theological reflection supported by the particular pluralist research program I am proposing is interreligious dialogue, which is portrayed in figure 1.2 below. Understanding what I mean requires an explanation of the diagram using a number of bullet points. I shall then bring these bullet points into a coherent, interrelated discussion in the following section followed by a conclusion in process.

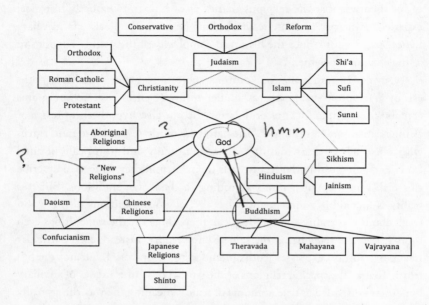

Figure 1.2: Model of a Pluralist Research Program

According to Alfred North Whitehead, creativity is "the category of the ultimate," meaning "the universal of universals characterizing ultimate matters of fact," a process by which "the universe disjunctively becomes the one actual occasion, which is the universe conjunctively." In the process, "the many become one and are increased by one."[16] As metaphysically ultimate, all things and events, in Whitehead's language all actual occasions of experience and societies of actual occasions of experience, at every moment of space-time—past, present, future—are actual instances of this universal creative process, including God, whom Whitehead believed was the chief example of the creative advance. As metaphysically ultimate, creativity has no boundaries, which is symbolized in Figure 1.2 by the empty spaces occupied by the circle and the boxes.

16. Whitehead, *Process and Reality*, 31–33.

But to be actual, creativity must be ingredient in an actual occasion or in societies of actual occasions. According to Whitehead, God is not an exception to the metaphysical principles at work in existence. Indeed, God is the chief instance of these principles. The circle upon which I have written "God," and which John Hick calls "the Real," occupies the center of the diagram. Of course, God's reality is not limited by conventional boundaries since, according to Whitehead, God is ingredient in the becoming of all things and events in the creative advance of the universe. My choice of "God" to designate the central referent in the diagram is a reflection of my training in theology and history of religions. Although it is open to criticism, "God" seems an appropriate descriptive designation of the referent of religious experience wherever it occurs. Thus while I do intend to employ this term in a generic sense, I also realize that as neutrally as I try to employ it, "God" carries Western and perhaps even theistic connotations that my not be fully adequate to the experiences of non-theistic religious persons. How one names what Hick calls "the Real" or Mircea Eliade called "the Sacred" will certainly constrain how one understands this reality. Even so, provided one is careful, "God" can be employed as a generic designation for the referent of religious experience, practice, and traditions. While I realize that this idea is open to the charge that it posits a "common ground" that often creates a debilitating relativism because it explains by explaining away real religious diversity and difference, persons who make this claim also invest themselves in interreligious dialogue. How this dialogue is possible without reference to a sacred reality that transcends all the particular religious traditions—however it is named—is not often clear. My point is that anyone who affirms interreligious dialogue as a practice tacitly implies that there *is* a common referent to which the collective religious traditions and experiences of humanity point, and it serves no purpose to deny it.[17] This constitutes the hard core of my pluralist research program. The specific research problem is how to indicate this common referent more specifically without explaining away the real convergences, incommensurablities, and diversity that constitute pluralism of the world's religious traditions. An equally important problem of my research program is how to avoid the trap of debilitating relativism.

The boxes surrounding the circle bear the name of some of the major religious traditions. I have included the best-known traditions and have left others out, i.e., Zoroastrianism, because I wanted to keep the diagram as

17. For a more complete response to the criticism of "common ground" notions of religious pluralism, see Ingram, *Wrestling with the Ox*, 172–74.

simple as possible, yet still specify the theoretical structure of my research program. In actual practice, one would have to include Zoroastrianism since its monotheism is historically connected to Jewish, Christian, and Islamic monotheism. My primary intention is to portray the various religious traditions as auxiliary hypotheses which form the protective belt surrounding the hard core. Each box is connected to "God" by an unbroken line representing my hypotheses that each of humanity's religious traditions refer to real, but historically and culturally limited experiences of the Sacred. The implication is that no particular religious tradition can claim universal validity or absolute truth for all human beings regarding the Sacred to which they all refer.

The broken lines linking Judaism, Christianity, and Islam are meant to indicate that these three monotheistic traditions have shared history, culture, teachings, and practices. The broken lines linking Islam with Sikhism and Hinduism with Sikhism represents the origins of Sikh tradition in Guru Nanak's teachings, which sought to harmonize aspects of Islam and Hinduism into a synthesis as a means of overcoming Hindu-Islamic violence. The broken lines linking Chinese Religions and Buddhism and Chinese Religions and Japanese Religions indicate the influence of Buddhism in Chinese religious thought and practice on such movements as Neo-Confucianism, as well as the influence of Buddhism in the religious history of Japan and its influence on Shinto and as the primary vehicle by which Confucianism and Daoism were introduced to Japan. The broken line linking Daoism and Confucianism indicate the fact that in the experience of most Chinese persons, Daoist and Confucian tradition do not function as distinct traditions. Finally, the broken line linking Shi'a, Sunni, and Sufi forms of Islam indicate that these three forms of Islam assert the defining character of the practice of Islam for all Muslims, the intention to "surrender to the will of God," but in their own distinctive ways, as well as the fact that Sufism is practiced within both Sunni and Shi'a communities.

The boxes surrounding the major religious traditions represent various sub-traditions within each of the major religious traditions. Thus Orthodox, Conservative, and Reform Judaism are themes and variations on three thousand years of Jewish history and experience. Orthodox religious experience, Conservative religious experience, and Reform religious experience constitute the data supporting Jewish teaching about the Sacred and its practices. Likewise Orthodox, Roman Catholic, and Protestant forms of Christianity constitute data supporting two thousand years Christian experience of the Sacred, as do Sunni, Shi'a, and Sufi versions of Islam constitute data for the truth and practice of Islamic monotheism. Daoism, Confucianism, and Buddhism are the data for Chinese religious experience, while the Theravada, Mahayana, and Vajrayana traditions are data for Buddhist teaching and practice.

By "data," I mean the religious experience of persons who participate in the various movements within the major religious traditions throughout their histories. Of course, scientific data and the data of religious experience are not identical. For one thing, the data that supports scientific theory is public, falsifiable, experimentally repeatable, closely tied to theory expressed mathematically, and is more often than not unrelated to ordinary human experiences of the world. The data of religious experience, while closely related to doctrine and teaching, is not experimentally repeatable, and carries a subjectivity not easily, if ever, open to empirical observation in the way that physical "facts" seem to be in the natural sciences. Nevertheless, the data of religious experience supports the teachings of the various religious traditions as differing referents to the Sacred. Otherwise persons would not be practicing these traditions.

APPLICATION OF THE PROPOSED RESEARCH PROGRAM

The Hard Core: The Sacred

In its application, the pluralist research program does not constitute a theological research program because it is not concerned with testing the validity of specific normative claims or with defending a particular religious tradition as the most accurate representation of the Sacred. As Murphy argues, specific theological traditions within, say, Christianity, can be viewed as competing interpretations of the hard core of Christian tradition, the incarnation.[18] In this sense, theological research programs tend to be more concerned with normative questions regarding the validity and truth of specific doctrines and practices within a specific religious tradition then the discipline of history of religions, which is focused on more descriptive issues. That is, more or less, theology is typically concerned with "what ought I believe and practice?" while history of religions is typically concerned with "what has been believed and practiced by religious human beings no matter where you find them?" Of course in actual practice, historians of religion are often involved in normative issues, as I shall be in this book, while theology must establish its

18. Murphy, *Theology in an Age of Scientific Reasoning*, 199–207; and Murphy and Ellis, *On the Moral Nature of the Universe*, chap. 8.

normative conclusions on the facts of religious experience revealed by history of religions.

Unlike a theological research program, my proposal is a history of religions research program that I think has normative implications for the theological and philosophical reflection that occurs in particular religious traditions, but is not itself a means for deciding whether, for example, Pannenberg's theological program is more adequate to Christian experience than Whiteheadian process theology. In fact, I think this is not the case, but I would not apply my pluralist research program to justify the claims of process theology over against Pannenberg. Furthermore, as a Christian historian of religions, I can only try to specify the implications for Christian theological reflection about the most appropriate way to interrelate with the world's religions. A Buddhist, Muslim, Hindu, or Jew accepting this research program would, I suspect, draw different normative conclusions in relating their particular traditions to the world's religions.

I have named the hard core of this research program "God," primarily because I cannot think of another adequate designation. What I intend by "God," however, is based on my interpretation of Whitehead's conception of God. Three aspects of Whitehead's cosmology are germane to my proposal. First, as I briefly noted above, is the category of creativity, which Whitehead described as the "universal of universals," meaning that process by which every individual entity in this universe—the "disjunctive diversity" of the universe—enters into complex unity—the "conjunctive" oneness of the universe. That is, the many actual occasions (all things and events at every moment of space-time) that constitutes the disjunctive diversity of the universe become one actual occasion, the universe conjunctively.[19] This implied for Whitehead that creativity is also the principle of novelty. All things and events are particular, novel entities distinct from every other entity in the universe that the universe experientially unifies. Yet since every actual occasion—every particular thing and event or societies of things and events—unifies the many that constitutes the universe itself in its own distinctive way according to its particular "subjective aim," creativity is a process that always introduces novelty into the content of the many things and events that constitute the universe conjunctively.[20]

19. Whitehead, *Process and Reality*, 161; also 141; and Whitehead, *Science and the Modern World*, 152–53; and Whithead, *Modes of Thought*, 31.

20. Ibid., 31–32.

What this implies is that the creative process at work in the universe has no independent existence apart from the actual things and events undergoing process. Therefore, as "categorically ultimate," all things and events undergo the universal process of creativity, including that actual occasion Whitehead called "God." All actual things and events, including God (the Sacred), are concrete instances of the "many becoming one and increased by one."

Second, while all things and events exemplify the process of creativity according to their own subjective aim, even if only trivially, Whitehead thought that God is the formative element, indeed the chief example of the creative process. Accordingly, Whitehead wrote of God's reality as bipolar, meaning constituted by two interdependent natures: an eternal "primordial nature" and a relationally processive "consequent nature." Creativity is ingredient in God's primordial nature, which Whitehead defined as the as "the active entertainment of all ideals, with the urge to their finite realization, each in its due season."[21] God's "consequent nature" is what God becomes as God affects and is affected by the multiplicity of past and present things and events at every moment of space-time as God unifies all things and events according to God's subjective aim that all things and events achieve maxim intensity and harmony of experience.[22] In other words, God's consequent nature is what God becomes as God experiences and interrelates with every entity in the universe, while God's primordial nature is an abstraction from the actual process of what God is in God's mutually processive consequent nature. Both natures are interdependent and mutually constitute what God "is" in God's own experience of the universe—and in the universe's experience of God.

Finally, God, according to Whitehead, is the source of novelty and order in existence. The source of novelty is God's primordial envisagement of pure possibilities together with an appetition that these possibilities be actualized in the universe, which is part of the initial aim given to all actual occasions of experience—which may or may not be taken into account by an occasion's subjective aim. Novelty as an actualization of new possibilities generally increases the enjoyment of experience because the variety of possibilities that are actualized in the universe add richness, texture, zest, and intensity to both God's and an occasion's experiences. It is in this sense that God is the source of novelty. However, there is a connection between order and novelty; the former's source is also God. Novel possibilities cannot be realized in the universe in simply any order; rather, some novel possibilities become real

21. *Process and Reality*, 343–44.

22. Ibid., 531–33.

only after others have been actualized. That is, at one stage certain novel possibilities are realized for the first time, and if they are repeated, they become part of the order of the world that contextualizes the actualization of future novel possibilities, and so on. Thus God is the source of order because: (1) order represents dominance of an ideal possibility that was at one time a novel element in the universe, so that God is the source of order by virtue of being the source of novelty; and (2) neither order nor novelty are intrinsically good, but instrumental to the one intrinsic good, which is the "enjoyment of intense experience."

Translating the above aspects of Whitehead's conception of God into the pluralist research program I am proposing, the Sacred is the source of order and novelty in the universe to which the particular religious traditions of the universe refer in their distinctive experiences, teachings, and practices, named differently by each tradition. Some religious traditions have emphasized (i.e., "prehended") the non-personal dimensions of the Sacred as ineffable, meaning beyond the ability of language—definition, doctrine, symbols—to fully grasp and conceptually express, e.g., the ineffability of Brahman in Upanishadic Hinduism or "Emptying" (śūnyatā) in Mahayana Buddhism or the Dao (the Way) in Daoist tradition. Included in these examples are mystical traditions such as Sufism and Jewish Kabbalah, as well as Christian mystical theology. Persons who participate in these traditions seek to experience a connection between themselves and the Sacred conceived as non-personally transcendent to, yet immanent within, all finite things and events through such disciplines as Yoga, meditation, and, in monotheistic tradition, contemplative prayer.

The vast majority of human beings have experienced (i.e., "prehended") the Sacred through a range of specific deities. Judging from the Paleolithic cave paintings in the Grotto of Lascaux in France, experience of the Sacred as a personal deity or set of deities with whom one is in relationship probably represents the most archaic expression of religious experience. Yet no one has ever encountered the Sacred as a deity "in general," or for that matter the Sacred as non-personal "in general." We never experience anything "in general," but only "in particular," always wrapped in historically and culturally situated images and symbols. For as there are different ways of being human and of participating in history, so it is that within the contexts of history and culture the presence of the Sacred as personal (or non-personal) is experienced differently. Christians encounter the Sacred as personal through stories of the life, death, and resurrection of the historical Jesus confessed to be the Christ. Christians in faith trust and bet their lives on these stories about the salvific relationship between human beings and God the Father and the Father's continuing work in the world through the Holy Spirit. Similarly, Jews bet their lives on the gift of Yahweh's Torah ("Instructions") and the resulting covenant between Jews and their Lord through Moses on Mount Sinai. Muslims surrender their wills (*islam*) to Allah, "the God," as recited by the Prophet Mohammed in the *Qur'an*, "the Book wherein there is no doubt," wherein Muslims believe is recorded the "straight way" of humanity's most complete religion. In Hindu devotional faith, the Sacred is experienced as Siva, Vishnu, Kali, Krishna, and Rama—in as many forms of Brahman as you please. Mahayana Buddhists, perhaps the majority, encounter the Dharma beyond name and form masked by a multiplicity of Bodhisattvas. Aboriginal people encounter the Sacred personified in wind, rain, mountains, lakes, rivers, sun, moon, stars, and the natural forces of growth and decay.

Still, there is always something non-personal about personalized forms of the Sacred as deities. It is not just that the deities often interrelate with nature and human beings non-personally—Jesus noticed that like rainfall, God's love for creation is disinterested and falls on the just and the unjust, so don't take it personally. Images of deities also reveal, even in the experiences of theistic forms of religious experience, that the Sacred is infinitely beyond the scope of human understanding and cultural and historical perspective. Yet, as both the non-theistic and theistic religious ways of humanity teach, just because we cannon know *everything* about the Sacred does not mean we cannot know *something*, since according to this version of pluralism, the Sacred is always interacting with the particulars of the universe as the source of ordered novelty.[23]

The Auxiliary Hypotheses: Humanity's Religious Traditions

The central question of the pluralist research program is, how *should* we understand the facts of religious pluralism and engage in interreligious encounter so that everyone has not only the right to speak, but also genuine ability to hear what is spoken? This is not an easy question, but the view I am proposing assumes as a start the existence of a common referent to which all the religious traditions of humanity point in their own historically-culturally contextualized ways. It seems to me that any notion of interreligious dialogue must assume a common referent, sometimes called a "common ground,"

23. For a more developed discussion of experience of the Sacred as non-personal and personal, see Ingram, *Wrestling with the Ox*, 76–86.

underlying the diversity of humanity's religious experience and history. As a process thinker, "common ground" is troublesome to me because this term seems to imply an unchanging substantial "essence," a notion contrary to Whiteheadian metaphysics and the natural sciences as well as human experience. But the religious traditions are in reference to something that each names differently according to her particular history of encounter with this referent. I have chosen to call this referent "God" and sometimes "the Sacred," but several other names for this referent have been proposed: the "common essence" of Arnold Toynbee; the object of "universal faith" posited by Wilfred Cantwell Smith and Bernard Lonergan; the "common mystical center" proposed by Thomas Merton, or the "object of ultimate concern" in Tillich's understanding of faith.[24]

However, numerous critics think that positing anything common between the religious traditions of humanity as a basis of dialogue and theological reflection is unwarranted and dangerous. Philosophers like Francis Schüssler Fiorenza and Richard Rorty are troubled by what they perceive as "objectivism" and "foundationalism." By this they mean the conviction that there must be some permanent ahistorical essence or framework to which we can finally appeal in determining the nature of rationality, knowledge, truth, reality, or religious experience—which both think is a highly inappropriate "modernist" attitude in our current "post-modern" age. Rather than looking for a common ground above or beyond the plurality of religious traditions, Fiorenza and Rorty enjoin us to accept the notion that all knowledge is "theory-laden." Different religions are different "plausibility structures" so that every particular religious tradition is plausible only within its own "language game." There can in principle, Fiorenza and Rorty argue, exist no common referent point upon which to stand to assess the meaning and truth claims made within each of the religious traditions. Different religious traditions are, in other words, "incommensurable."[25]

Christian theologians like John Cobb and Raimundo Panikkar are also highly critical of "objectivism." They warn that the search for any universal should be abandoned. Panikkar's critique is particularly harsh. A genuine

---

24. See Toynbee, *An Historian's Approach to Religion*, 261–83; Smith, *The Meaning and End of Religion*, chaps. 6–7; Smith, *Faith and Belief*; Lonergan, *Method in Theology*, 1–24; Stace, *Mysticism and Philosophy*; Merton, *The Asian Journals of Thomas Merton*, 309–17; and Tillich, *Dynamics of Faith*, 1–40.

25. See Fiorenza, *Foundational Theology*, 283–311; and Rorty, *Philosophy and the Mirror of Nature*.

religious pluralism, he thinks, cannot and should not imagine a universal system of thought. For him, a pluralist "system" is a contradiction, and the "incommensurability of ultimate systems is unbridgeable."[26] Likewise, Cobb is critical of John Hick, Wilfred Cantwell Smith, Paul Knitter, and me. He thinks that looking for something common to all religions traditions is to abandon religious pluralism to ahistorical reductionism. It is better, Cobb writes, simply to be open, which he thinks is inhibited unnecessarily if we state in advance what all religious traditions have in common. The danger is, Cobb rightly points out, that we might miss what is genuinely different, and therefore what is genuinely challenging, in religious traditions other than our own.[27]

In fact, Cobb regards this danger as so likely that he suggests that there is no one "ultimate" within or beyond the world's religious traditions. Rather, he thinks there might be "multiple ultimates" behind all religious traditions and that religious pluralists like Huston Smith, Wilfred Cantwell Smith, Hick, Knitter, and me are afraid to face this possibility.[28] I am forced to admit that proposing that religious traditions are similar to auxiliary hypotheses that function like a protective belt in their particular reference to the hard core of my research program does indeed run the risk of imperialistically imposing my theoretical construction on religious traditions other than my own. Furthermore, I am fully aware that many serious Buddhists, Hindu, Muslims, Jews, Christians, Sikhs, and other religious persons will not wish to speak about their experiences mediated through their own particular religious traditions and practice as a common referent to which all religious traditions symbolically point.

Still, even as critics forcefully warn against the pitfalls of objectivism, they just as forcefully warn against radical skepticism based on a debilitating relativism that so locks the religious traditions of humanity within their own particular language games and plausibility structures as to make dialogue between them impossible. Fiorenza, Rorty, Panikkar, and Cobb paradoxically assert the possibility of dialogue between the world's incommensurable religious traditions. In doing so, they look for a path between objectivism and relativism by asserting that even though there exists no preestablished common referent or "ground" among the world's religious traditions, persons

26. Panikkar, "The Jordan, the Tiber, and the Ganges," 110.

27. Cobb, "Beyond Pluralism."

28. Ibid. See also Cobb, "Buddhist Emptiness and the Christian God"; and Cobb, *Christ in a Pluralistic Age*, 202–29.

inhabiting different religious traditions can still, and should, talk to and understand one another.

How this is possible is not often clear. Cobb and Panikkar simply trust the *praxis* of communication to reveal common experiences, shared problems, and shared viewpoints and plunge into conversation. They believe that whatever common ground emerges in the dialogue can suffice to overcome incommensurability (e.g., between *śūnyatā* and God in Cobb's theology) and lead to mutual understanding and "mutual transformation."[29] Similarly, even as Panikkar disavows universal theories of religion and the idea of a common ground shared by all religious persons, he still invokes a single "aspiration" or "inspiration" that in some unexplained way unifies all religious traditions.

What Cobb and Panikkar have apprehended is that different religious traditions cannot be ultimately different, as, say, apples are different from granite, in an interdependent, interconnected universe. If they are, how or why or should or could interreligious dialogue even happen? My point is, anyone affirming the value of interreligious dialogue as a "practice" (*praxis*) tacitly affirms that there *does* exist a referent that bonds the religious traditions together, even in their differences, and it serves no purpose to deny it. The problem is, how do we indicate this referent explicitly? My proposal for a pluralist research program is a theoretical framework for making the implicit assumption of interreligious dialogue—the existence of a referent to which the religious traditions of humanity point—explicit.

I have in past publications tried to be explicit about what I perceive to be the referent underlying the plurality of humanity's religious faith and practice.[30] Many historians of religions refer to this referent as "the Sacred." All references to the Sacred—even "the Sacred"—are metaphorical in nature. I do not claim that this metaphor or any other metaphor e.g., "God," is the only one suitable for conceiving what the referent to which humanity's religious traditions point. But whatever the metaphor, what it points to is a reality that transcends verbal limitations. So while it is possible, or even likely that using "the Sacred" or "God" as a metaphor for naming the referent for humanity's religious traditions might be a mistake, what is not likely is the non-existence of a referent to which religious traditions of humanity point in their distinctive, historically contextualized ways.

---

29. Cobb, "Buddhist Emptiness and the Christian God," 86–90.

30. See Ingram, *Wrestling with the Ox*, chap. 2.

The Question of Evidence

In the natural sciences, a research program requires evidence supporting its coherence and fruitfulness, meaning its ability to experimentally predict and confirm conclusions coupled with its capability for accounting for unexpected, anomalous data the hard core did not originally predict, but which can be incorporated into the program through changes in the structure of its auxiliary hypotheses in ways that are coherent with the hard core. The question is, what counts as evidence and how does evidence relate to experience? In the natural sciences, the gathering of data subjected to experimental verification supports conclusions that are falsifiable. Furthermore, the foci of scientific investigation are the physical relationships that explain natural phenomena. The explanatory power of a scientific research program originates in the narrowness of its focus, which means that most scientific conclusions have little direct bearing on how human beings actually experience the world.

For example, one of Newton's discoveries was his laws of motion, which assume that the natural tendency of a body is to keep moving forever. But our actual experience of moving bodies on planet Earth is that they always come to a stop, usually rather quickly, unless we keep pushing them. According to Newton's laws of motion, the explanation of this paradox is that friction acts to prevent a body from doing what its natural tendency dictates. According to Murphy, this is an example of a "broken symmetry" because the conservation of energy one would expect to see in a freely moving body, described mathematically in Newton's equations, is not what we actually observe in practice. So the true nature of motion is hidden by the way a body empirically, that is, actually moves.[31] In this sense, Newton's laws of motion are as counter-intuitive as the non-locality of quantum events in contemporary physics because they do not easily conform to our everyday experience.

Of course, the evidence supporting the pluralist research program I am proposing is incapable of experimental repetition. Furthermore, evidence supporting a non-scientific research program is mostly experiential and historical, socially and culturally contextual, often intensely private while simultaneously communal and non-repeatable, and subject to a number of philosophical, historical, and theological interpretations over time. This means that a theological research program, as well as the pluralist research program I am proposing, is concerned with a wider body of experience than scientific research programs: individual and communal religious experience, ethical experience, philosophical questions, and social justice issues that scientists intentionally

31. Murphy, *On the Moral Nature of the Universe*, 43.

exclude from scientific inquiry. So what does constitute evidence in support of my particular pluralist research program?

While my own particular experiences cannot be universalized, I shall begin with reference to how certain aspects of my scholarly work in history of religions seems to me to constitute evidence pointing to a referent common to humanity's religious experience. Since other scholars in my field have reported similar experiences, what follows is, I believe, supporting evidence for the fruitfulness of pluralism as a research program. In my case, study of and dialogue with non-Christian traditions and persons have deepened my own understanding of Christian faith and practice. I have thereby learned that experience of the Sacred is pretty much a now-you-see-it-now-you-don't affair, even for scholars. An insight flashes through a text or a conversation or a ritual practice, then dissolves into intellectual and emotional fog. But I have read Lord Krishna's instruction to Arjuna in the *Bhagavad-gita* about the numerous incarnations of Brahman into an infinite pluralism of deities, and this has helped me comprehend the possibilities of God's incarnation in the historical Jesus as the Christ that unifies the pluralism of Christian faith and practice. I have read Buddhist Pure Land texts through Shinran's eyes and have apprehended with him the "other-powered" grace of Amida Buddha's universal compassion, and this has helped me comprehend the grace of God that Augustine, Aquinas, and Luther discovered in Paul's writings when they thought and wrote about faith. I have read how Elijah sitting alone in a cave saw the back side of God passing in review, and that has led me to see how the One God experienced by Mohammed sitting alone in a cave can be closer to a person than a jugular vain; this has clarified for me Christian monotheistic experience of God's interdependent transcendence and immanence. These experiences, and others emerging from my scholarship, have often stunned me to silence. They constitute examples of partial evidence that the religious traditions of humankind point to, but never fully reveal, a common referent, which I have named "the Sacred" in my work in history of religions and which I name "God" when I am engaged in specifically Christian theological reflection. The reality of this referent is more than can be named by any specific religious tradition because whatever this reality is, it conceals itself even as it reveals itself with eye-catching nonchalance. Humanity's religious traditions reveal as much as they conceal, and much depends on the questions asked and the assumptions through which the Sacred is experienced and interpreted.

There also exists public evidence in support of the pluralist research program, by which I mean experiences shared in common, even though such public experiences are tweaked and interpreted according to the particu-lar communal traditions that filter these experiences to their participants. A meaningful way to conceive of this evidence is by means of the "bridge" metaphor suggested by Paul Knitter in the preface of *The Myth of Christian Uniqueness*.[32] One can think of the pluralist research program as a bridge by which one can dialogically cross into the varied traditions constituting the world's religious traditions, while avoiding exclusivist religious claims (all re-ligious traditions other than my own are false) and inclusivist religious claims (to the degree that religious traditions other than my own look like my own, they are vehicles of truth).

Issues of relativism constitute one such "historical-cultural bridge." In fact, this particular "bridge" is the starting point for most reflection on the nature of pluralism and is built on compelling awareness of historical consciousness. Historical consciousness is awareness of the historical-cultural limitations of all knowledge and religious beliefs, coupled with the difficulty of judging the truth claims of another culture or religious tradition on the basis of one's own. This is why Gordon Kaufman claims that a necessary condition for interreligious dialogue is that the participants recognize the his-torical relativity of all religious beliefs and practices and thereby abandon all claims of being the only or the highest form of religious belief and practice.[33] John Hick notes that if any religious tradition is going to make claims of superiority, it must do so on the basis of "an examination of the facts," that is, on some form of empirical data available to all. Hick believes that such data would have to be found in the ability of a particular religious tradition to promote the welfare of humanity better than other religious traditions. He doe not think such data is available. He writes: "it seems impossible to make the global judgment that any religious tradition has contributed more good or less evil, or a more favorable balance of good over evil, than the others . . . As vast complex totalities, the world religious seem to be more or less on a par with each other. None can be singled out as manifestly superior."[34]

It is not only the fact that our religious perceptions are historically relative—"relational" is a better word—but also that the object of religious experience is, when all is said and done, Mystery beyond all forms, exceeding every grasp of it. This is the "mystical bridge" that is attested to by all religious traditions, so that the ineffability of the Sacred Mystery demands religious

32. Knitter, "Preface," in *The Myth of Christian Uniqueness*, ix–xii.
33. Kaufman, "Religious Diversity, Historical Consciousness, and Christian Theology."
34. Hick, "The Non-Absoluteness of Christianity," 30.

pluralism and forbids any single religious tradition from possessing the only or final truth about the Sacred. Wilfred Cantwell Smith was a champion of this " theological-mystical bridge"[35] until the day he died. He used the notion of idolatry to state why pluralism should be the attitude governing inter-religious dialogue. "Idolatry" describes not only other religions traditions, but also any attempt to absolutize one's own. Because "Christianity has been our idol," he writes, Christians have too easily given in to the temptation to equate Christianity with God by making Christian faith, like God, absolute and final. Repenting of this idolatry means to cease all exclusive or inclusive claims and to be open to the "possible equality of other religious traditions with one's own."[36] Raimundo Panikkar and Stanley Samartha are Christians who draw on Hinduism to lay a mystical foundation for Cantwell Smith's warnings against Christian idolatry.[37] For them, the Sacred is the Ultimate Mystery and is as ineffable (*neti-neti* or "not this-not that," of Upanishadic teaching) as it is real. All religious traditions reflect, as they participate in, the Mystery in their own limited and unique ways, but none can own it or claim absolute truth about this Mystery. Panikkar is particularly insistent on the limitations of reason. For him, the Sacred is not only ineffable, but also radically pluralistic. So too is all reality, as Whitehead suggests. Thus Panikkar concludes that most pluralist thinkers do not really know what radical plural-ism means. Pluralism tells us that there is no "one" that can be imposed on "many"; there will always be "one" and "many," which means there will always be differences and disagreements about the one Sacred reality named differ-ently in the plurality of the many religious traditions of humanity. Therefore, pluralism does not allow for a universal religious system. The impossibility of a universal religious system is, for Panikkar, a revelation of the nature of the Sacred itself. Accordingly, a pluralist research program should not be un-derstood as a universal system, but a hermeneutics of interreligious dialogue that explores what the religious traditions of the world as auxiliary hypotheses have revealed about the Sacred.

The need to promote justice points to what Knitter calls the "ethico-religious bridge." Two considerations in this regard require specification. First, the ethical principles and practices of the major world religions seem

35. Knitter, preface, x.

36. Smith, "Idolatry in Comparative Perspective."

37. See Samartha, "The Cross and the Rainbow: Christ in a Multireligious Culture"; and Panikkar, "The Jordan, The Tiber, and the Ganges: Three Kairological Moments of Christic Self-Consciousness."

universal in their focus on compassion, love, honesty, and justice. For example, the practice of compassion that stems from Buddhist experience interpreted through its doctrine of interdependence can easily be affirmed by Christians, Jews, and Muslims even though each tradition nuances these moral values according to their specific worldviews. Second, issues of justice that all human beings face are not religion-specific. Gender injustice, racial injustice, social and economic injustice, violence, and environmental injustice are not Christian, Buddhist, or Muslim issues. They affect all human beings regardless of religious affiliation or lack of religious affiliation. The fact that persons of different religious traditions experience injustice and can and have worked together in what is now called "social engagement" to promote justice constitutes strong evidence for the research program I am proposing. Such socially engaged dialogue does not require that religious persons share common worldviews and practices. Yet the differing worldviews and practices of the major world religions promote social engagement with the forces of injustice running riot in human communities.

For example, Marjorie Suchocki and Rosemary Ruether have clarified how traditional understandings of Christian tradition as the supreme religion have led to "an outrageous and absurd religious chauvinism." They think that holding Christian tradition as the norm for judging all other religious traditions is just as exploitive as sexist assertions of male experience as the universal norm of humanity that creates injustice against women.[38] Knitter goes so far as to say that given the shared moral intuitions of the religions of the world, the starting point and guide for the practice of interreligious dialogue should be something like a "preferential option" for those persons most in need as the primary context for the meeting of the world religions.

Evidence supporting pluralism as a research paradigm is not merely a matter of similarities in doctrines, teachings, experiences engendered by practices, or common ethical principles that cut across the boundaries of specific religious traditions. There are also differences between the religious traditions of the world, differences that express non-negotiationables that define the unique character of that tradition. For example, Christian experience and teaching regarding the incarnation is not something Christians can compromise in the practice of Christian faith and still meaningfully participate in a distinctively Christian faith community. Likewise, Islamic monotheism is a call not to reduce God to that which cannot be God and surrender to it,

38. See Suchocki, "Religious Pluralism from a Feminist Perspective"; and Rosemary Radford Ruether, "Feminism and Jewish-Christian Dialogue."

which means no Muslim can accept any form of the Christian doctrine of incarnation and remain within the House of Islam. Buddhist non-theism and Jewish, Christian, and Islamic monotheism are incommensurable. Even as reading the *Bhagavad-gita* still clarifies Christian experience of the incarnation for me, Christian teaching of a single incarnation of God in a particular human life is incommensurable with the *Gita*'s notion of the many incarnations of Brahman in the deities of Hindu experience and teaching. What Buddhist's mean by Awakening is not identical with what Christian tradition means by salvation. The list goes on.

But a pluralist research program need not assume that all religious doctrines and beliefs teach the same things. One need not assume that similar experiences and ideas that cut across religious boundaries possess more evidentiary value supporting pluralism than the non-negotiationables that separate particular religious traditions from one another. In this regard, three points can be made. First, incommensurable teachings, practices, and experiences need not always imply contradiction. Often, differences between religious persons and the communities they represent are complementary. For example, Buddhist practice is thoroughly grounded in non-theism. Yet Christian experience of God as personal also includes experience of God as non-personal, as in, for example, Christian mystical theology and practice. Likewise, Buddhist non-theism includes elements of devotional experience and practice in Pure Land Buddhism that seem in many ways experientially similar to Christian theistic experience. While I as a Lutheran think the incarnation points to how God has always worked in the universe, and continues to work, the incarnation of God in the historical Jesus does not exhaust the reality of God, which means the faith and practices of non-Christians can teach me lessons I need to understand.

Second, the existence of incommensurable teaching and practices in the world's religious traditions should surprise no one. If my pluralist research program bears correspondence to reality, the religious traditions of humanity are best understood as limited, historically and culturally conditioned means by which human beings have grasped and been grasped by the Sacred. According to most of humanity's religious traditions, the Sacred is beyond the categories of thought and speech. That is, it is an ineffable Mystery that can be glimpsed and experienced contextually in the pluralism of human culture and history, but only partially and incompletely. But just because the Sacred as it is cannot be known completely or expressed in any final way does not mean that human beings cannot say and know something about the Sacred.

Finally, incommensurable teachings may be, and often are, radically contradictory, as exemplified by Buddhist non-theism and Jewish, Christian, and Islamic monotheism. To Muslims surrendering (*'islam*) to the call of the Qur'an not to reduce God to that which cannot be God, the Christian doctrine of the Trinity can only seem like "idolatry" (*shirk*). Christians who apprehend God incarnated in the life, death, and resurrection of the historical Jesus as the norm of faith must be in disagreement with Muslim teaching that Jesus, while an extraordinary prophet, can never be a redeemer. In such instances, either both doctrines are false—neither corresponds to reality, or "the way things really are as opposed to what we wish things to be"—or one is true or at least truer than its opposite. But how does one decide given the fact that religious persons faithful to their traditions can only relate to other traditions from the perspective of their own traditions? Human beings seem unable to be religious "in general," but only "in particular."

In reflecting on this difficult question, it helps to remember that the pluralist research program does not presuppose that all religious doctrines and practices are equally true or that all religions traditions are equally valid. It's very difficult to argue that White supremacy is a valid form of Christianity or that Islamic extremism and terrorism are authentic expressions of the Qur'an's call that human beings live in peaceful community with one other and with nature. In these examples, distinguishing truth from falsehood is rather easy. But deciding whether Buddhist non-theism or Christian monotheism is a truer account of the Sacred that constitutes the hard core of the pluralist research program is another matter. While according to this program it is reasonable to argue that the world's religious traditions point to a common referent, it is not reasonable to assert that these traditions are equally true or that one religious tradition is truer than all the rest. No religious person has enough knowledge or experience to make such a judgment. We may affirm, for example, that a particular doctrine or practice or religious tradition is the best account of the Sacred *for us*; we cannot do so for someone else. In other words, the pluralist research program requires a confessional approach to theological-philosophical reflection that is expressed through the practice of interreligious dialogue.

In this regard, another point requires clarification. The natural sciences need to be brought into the practice of interreligious dialogue as a contributing partner since in this post-modern age, all religious persons must practice their faith in the context of what the natural sciences are revealing about the physical structures of the universe. What the sciences are revealing about the physical structures of reality both challenges and, if approached with care and sensitivity, deepens religious faith and practice wherever found. According to the Whiteheadian perspective assumed by this essay, the Sacred, however it is named, is immanent in the very physical process of the universe. When taken together with the comprehensive explanatory power of the natural sciences, the conclusion must be that the Sacred is "in, with, and under" the universe's unfolding natural processes of which the Sacred is the transcendent reality beyond name and form holding all name and form together in a unity supporting incredible pluralism. Some of this pluralism constitutes the religious traditions of humanity.

A CONCLUDING POSTSCRIPT

When I was teaching at Simpson College in Indianola, Iowa, one of my students stopped by my home for help in writing a paper assignment I had given him. He was from Kenya and he was Muslim. There were not many black people or Muslims living in Indianola in those days, and my four-year-old daughter, Gail, had never seen a black person. As Mohammed and I were talking, my daughter climbed on his lap and rubbed her hand across his face and said, "Daddy, why won't it come off?"

"Ask Mohammed," I said.

When she did, Mohammed answered, "Because this is the way God made me."

"Why," my daughter asked.

"Because God loves wondrous diversity."

The lesson from my Muslim student was not only for my daughter. To me, it gave new meaning to the Prologue of the Gospel of John. From a young and gifted Muslim student I learned how to recognize that it was God's outgoing expressive Word (*Logos*) in creation that was all the time present incognito in the universe and "made flesh" in the world in Jesus—that is, made explicit and manifest in a human being. This ancient insight both preserves Christian perceptions of the uniqueness of the historical Jesus as the Christ and at the same time recognizes fully that God's Word, God's Self-expression, is likely manifested in all times and in all places in other religious traditions and cultures through their own symbolic and historical resources. One need not engage in a contest to determine which religious tradition is superior.

2

The Structure Buddhist-Christian Conceptual Dialogue

CHRISTIAN CONCEPTUAL DIALOGUE WITH BUDDHISM

The focus of conceptual dialogue is doctrinal, theological, and philosophical. It concerns a religious tradition's collective self-understanding and worldview. In conceptual dialogue, Buddhists and Christians compare theological and philosophical formulations on such questions as ultimate reality, human nature, suffering and evil, the role of Jesus in Christian faith, the role of the Buddha in Buddhist practice, and what Christians and Buddhists can conceptually learn from one another. Historically, Christians have encountered Buddhists since the first century CE.[1] Yet until the sixteenth-century Jesuit missions to China and Japan led by Mattaeo Ricci and Francis Xavier, respectively, precise knowledge of Buddhist teachings and practices were generally inaccurate and uninformed. As knowledge of Buddhism gradually made its way into the West, Christian encounter with Buddhism was more monological than dialogical for cultural and historical reasons peculiar to both traditions. Serious Western attempts to understand Buddhism in its own terms did not begin until the emergence of scholarly research in the field of history of religions (*Religionswissenschaft*) in the nineteenth century, which provided the historical context for Christian

---

1. The first textual reference to Buddhism in Christian literary sources appears around the year 200 in the *Miscellany* (*Stromateis*) of Clement of Alexandria, who wished to show that Christian *gnosis* was superior to every other form of wisdom: "And there are in India those who follow the commandments of the Buddha, whom they revere as a God because of his immense holiness"; cited in Küng, *Christianity and the World Religions*, 307.

contemporary encounter with the world religions in general, and with Buddhism in particular.

Most Christian theological reflection on Buddhism was exclusivist in nature because its main purpose was to demonstrate the superiority of Christian faith and practice as the sole vehicle of humanity's salvation. Serious theological challenge to this agenda began to appear in the summer of 1980, when David Chappell organized the first "East-West Religions in Encounter" conference at the University of Hawaii. The structure of Christian theological reflection on Buddhism has since changed from an exclusivist monologue to dialogical encounter, at least in liberal circles of contemporary Catholic and Protestant thought. The initial "East-West Religions in Encounter" group is now permanently organized as the Society for Buddhist-Christian Studies (SBCS). This society and its journal, *Buddhist-Christian Studies*, have evolved into an important international forum for worldwide support of the continuing dialogue now occurring between Christians and Buddhists.

Contemporary Christian encounter with Buddhism reflects the pluralism of post-modern and, some would argue, post-Christian, cultural and religious diversity because Christian encounter with Buddhism, as is Buddhist encounter with Christianity, is itself pluralistic. This pluralism is rooted in the history of Christian encounter with the world religions since the first century, a history in which there have existed a limited number of theological options for considering other religious traditions. Most Christian responses were exclusivist and rejected non-Christian religions as idolatrous coupled with the goal of replacing them through the conversion of their followers. Hellenistic paganism was viewed in this way. Or the Greek and Roman philosophers could be seen as possessing limited goodness and truth, which is fulfilled and perfected in Christianity. The mainly inclusivist Christian response to Neoplatonism by the church fathers and mothers illustrates this possibility, where Christians sought to convert Neoplatonists to Christianity while at the same time preserving this tradition's attainments. Sometimes a non-Christian tradition was viewed as nonreligious, in which case it could be allowed to continue along side of Christianity. In the seventeenth century, Jesuit missionaries in China treated Confucianism in this way.

By the second half of the twentieth-century Christian theology of religions within some liberal circles took a new direction when many theologians recognized the validity of non-Christian religious traditions. Accordingly, much Christian scholarship on non-Christian religions focused on developing a neutral methodology for the comparative study of religions. Tolerance became a central theological virtue. Partly as a negative reaction to this trend, neo-orthodox writers reasserted theological exclusivism by claiming that Christian faith is not one religion among others, but is not a religion at all. For example, Karl Barth, Emile Brunner, and Dietrich Bonhoeffer defined "religion," including "Christian religion," as a human activity, whereas what is crucial in Christian faith is God's decisive action and response to the world through Jesus Christ. Responding to God's act in Christ is "faith," not "religion." Because of the influence of Protestant neo-orthodoxy following the Second World War, theology and history of religions developed independently of one another as specialized academic disciplines with little interdisciplinary contact.

In neo-orthodox theology, no salvation apart from explicit faith has usually meant commitment to doctrinal propositions, particularly the doctrine of justification by faith through grace alone. So when Barth wrote that Christian faith is not "religion" because "religion is unbelief," meaning "man's attempt to justify and sanctify himself before a capricious and arbitrary picture of God,"[2] he set the essentials of Protestant neo-orthodoxy's approach to Buddhism in particular and non-Christian religious traditions in general: no "religion," including Christianity understood as a "religion," has any truth that can lead persons to salvation because all "religions" are inventions by sinful human beings seeking to establish a saving relationship with God by means of their own contrivances. The opposite of "religion" is Christian faith, which is not a "religion" but a "witness" to a different reality, namely, "God's condescension to us" through Christ. Christian faith always rests on God's prior action of breaking into the conditions of existence through the life, death, and resurrection of the historical Jesus as the Christ. In regard to Buddhism, Barth once took note of the similarity between the doctrines of faith and grace in Christian and Japanese Pure Land Buddhist traditions. But he dismissed this aspect of Buddhist doctrine as an inferior expression of what Christians experience through faith in Christ.[3]

While it is clear that most Christians have understood that participation in Christian faith and practice is the exclusive means of salvation, this has not always implied the absence of God's saving action for non-Christians or the inability or unwillingness to incorporate truth perceived in non-Christians traditions into Christian self-understanding. But from the time of Constantine the Great (280?–337), when the church began transforming itself into a sacred institution claiming both religious and secular authority over the lives

2. Barth, "The Revelation of God and the Absolutism of Religion."

3. Ibid., 340–44.

of Christians and non-Christians, what is today called "theology of religions" in Christian circles took on a hard-line exclusivism: all human beings must become Christian in order to be in a saving relationship with God. This idea, later promulgated by the Council of Florence (1438–45) as the doctrine of "no salvation outside the church" (*extra ecclesiam nulla sallus*), is the classical form of Christian theological exclusivism. In pre-Vatican II Roman Catholic theology of religions, "no salvation outside the church" meant no salvation apart from participation in Catholic sacraments and ethical teachings. When the Second Vatican Council published the "Dogmatic Constitution of the Church" and the "Declaration of the Relationship of the Church to Non-Christian Religions" in 1964 and 1965 respectively, Roman Catholic theology of religions and its conversation with Buddhism took on a more inclusive character.

Barth's exclusivist theology of religions in particular, and Protestant neo-orthodox theology in general, did not take the world's religions seriously as objects of theological reflection. Nor did Catholic theology. But after the Second World War, voices arose within Protestant and Catholic circles that paid more critical attention to the world's religions. Two important transitional Protestant figures in this regard are Paul Tillich and Jürgen Moltmann, both of whom set important precedents for the development of theological encounter with Buddhism and other religious traditions.

After Tillich's encounter with important Buddhist philosophers in Japan and the publication of his *Christianity and the Encounter with the World's Religions*, he concluded that his "method of correlation" was inadequate for judging the truth of non-Christian traditions. Tillich's method of correlation, deeply influenced by Søren Kierkegaard's existentialist philosophy, asserted that the universal questions all human beings have about the meaning of existence are most completely answered by the Christian revelation. He did not seriously entertain the possibility that there might be more adequate Buddhist or Hindu or Islamic answers to these universal questions. But his experience in Japan taught him that there might be some questions and answers in Buddhist tradition that might correlate more adequately to the structures of existence than Christian answers to these same questions. Consequently, Tillich began reflecting on how Christian encounter with religious pluralism might deepen both Christian theology and Christian experience. Unfortunately, Tillich died before he could develop his evolving insights into a systematic theology of religions.[4]

4. Tillich, *Christianity and the Encounter with the World's Religions*; and Tillich, *Systematic Theology*, vol. 1, 3–68.

Similarly, Moltmann wrote of the need for Christian encounter with the world's religions as a means not only for Christian renewal, but the renewal of non-Christian religions as well. But before Christians can enter dialogue with non-Christians, two historic prejudices governing Christian interaction with the world's religions must be explicitly renounced: the absolutism of the church and the absolutism of Christianity. Moltmann's theology of religions is intentionally inclusivist. For him, faith as trust in God's actions for humanity and the entirety of existence, past, present, and future—not trust in theological or liturgical systems—makes dialogue with non-Christians not only possible, but theologically necessary because the reality Christians encounter in the life, death, and resurrection of the historical Jesus as the Christ has also encountered human beings through non-Christian experience and practice.[5]

Since conservative and fundamentalist Protestant theologians have taken an essentially exclusive stance toward the non-Christian religions, including Buddhism, the Protestant theologians cited in this chapter represent, in various ways, the liberal end of the Protestant theological spectrum that has followed the precedents set by Tillich's and Moltmann's encounter with the world religions. Post-Vatican II Roman Catholic theology of religions is marked by an inclusivist approach that gives Roman Catholic encounter with Buddhism more theological unity than generally found in liberal Protestant circles. The two most important contemporary voices of current Catholic theological reflection on religions pluralism are Karl Rahner and Hans Küng, whose theologies of religions provide the foundations for most contemporary Catholic theological encounter with Buddhism. Rahner's theology of religion is centered on his notion of "anonymous Christianity," according to which devout Buddhists, Muslims, Hindus, or Sikhs encounter the same reality Christians encounter through faith in Christ, only do not realize it. They are "anonymous Christians." Accordingly, the missionary task of the Church is to encourage anonymous Christians to become explicitly Christian through conversion to the Church's teachings and participation in its sacraments.[6]

Since Küng has been more intentionally engaged in Buddhist-Christian dialogue than Rahner, a fuller explanation of his encounter with Buddhism will be offered later in this chapter. For now, it will suffice to note that Küng's general theology of religions assumes that the world's religious traditions,

---

5. Moltmann, *The Church in the Power of the Spirit*, 151ff. Also see De Martino, trans., "Dialogue East and West."

6. Rahner, *Theological Investigations*, vol. 5, 131. Also see essays in other volumes of *Theological Investigations*, especially vols. 6, 9, 12, and 14.

by which he means all religious traditions other than Roman Catholicism, should be understood as "extraordinary ways of human salvation." The Catholic Church, however, is the "ordinary way." Therefore, persons may attain salvation through the particular religious traditions available to them in their historical and cultural circumstances, since God—whose fullest self-revelation is through Christ—is also at work in the extraordinary ways of non-Christian teachings and practices. But compared with the extraordinary ways of salvation, the ordinary way of the Church seems, in Küng's view, the fullest expression God's self-revelation through Christ. Since neither Küng nor Rahner evaluate non-Christian religious traditions as valid avenues to saving truth in their own right, but rather as "preparations for the gospel," the Church should undertake missionary efforts to non-Christians while simultaneously recognizing the truths of non-Christian traditions.[7]

Protestant neo-orthodox encounter with Buddhism is monological in nature because of the exclusivist structure of its theology. Post-Vatican II theology of religions is structurally inclusivist and is also thoroughly monological in its encounter with Buddhism. But since 1980, forms of Christian conceptual dialogue with Buddhism have emerged that have pushed the boundaries of Christian theological reflection in directions unimaginable before 1980. This has involved appropriating Buddhist doctrinal and philosophical traditions into Christian theology as a means of creatively transforming contemporary Christian thought and practice. Three Western theologians, two Protestant and one Roman Catholic, one historian of religions, and three Asian theologians will serve as examples of Christian writers pushing the boundaries of Christian theology of religions by their intentional appropriation of Buddhist thought into the structure of their theological reflection.

John B. Cobb Jr.

Few Protestant theologians have conceptually engaged Buddhism more systematically while incorporating Buddhist thought into their theologies than process theologian John Cobb, who is one of the first major Protestant theologians to appropriate the scholarship of history of religions, particularly in regard to Buddhism, as an object of his theological reflection. The foundation of his particular dialogue with Buddhism is a process he calls "passing beyond dialogue."[8] Passing beyond dialogue does not mean the practice of

7. Küng, *On Being a Christian*, 89–116.
8. Cobb, *Beyond Dialogue*, chap. 2.

ceasing dialogue, since theological reflection is itself a dialogical process. Rather, "passing beyond dialogue" names the process of continual theological engagement *in* dialogue as a contributive element of one's continued growth in Christian faith. Cobb assumes the same process will occur for Buddhists as well, who, faithful to Buddhist tradition, go beyond dialogue with Christian tradition.

For Cobb, dialogue is itself a theological practice that involves two interdependent movements: (1) in dialogue with Buddhists, Christians should intentionally leave the conventional boundaries of Christian tradition and enter into Buddhist thought and experience, (2) followed by a return to the home of Christian faith enriched, renewed, and "creatively transformed," which is the goal of "passing beyond dialogue." The purpose of interreligious dialogue for Christians is "creative transformation," defined as a process of critically appropriating whatever one has learned from dialogue into one's own faith and practice, whereby one's faith is challenged, enriched, and renewed. For Christians, the image of creative transformation is Christ, who explicitly provides a focal point of unity within which the many centers of meaning that characterize the present "post-Christian" age of religious pluralism are harmonized. Because he thinks that no truths can be contradictory if really true, Christians can and should be open to the "structures of existence" of the other "religious ways" of humanity.[9] But the appropriation of Buddhist doctrines into one's Christian theological reflection does not entail imposing Christian meanings foreign to Buddhist experience. Conceptual dialogue that leads to the creative transformation of Christian faith should falsify neither Christian nor Buddhist experience.

The specific forms of creative transformation that Cobb seeks in his particular dialogue with Buddhism are interrelated with his commitment to the process metaphysics of Alfred North Whitehead. For example, dialogue with Buddhism, he believes, can help Christians understand how inadequately theology has reflected on the nonsubstantial character of God and human selfhood. To make this point, he incorporates the Mahayana Buddhist doctrines of "emptying" (Sanskrit *śūnyatā*) and "non-self" (Sanskrit *anātman*) into his doctrine of God. What does Buddhist philosophy mean when it teaches that an event (for example, a moment of human experience) is "empty"? As Cobb accurately interprets this Buddhist teaching, "emptying" means: (1) that the experience is empty of substance, so that the moments of a person's experience are not unified by an enduring "I" remaining self-identical through time;

9. Cobb, *Christ in a Pluralistic Age*, 21, 58.

(2) the experience lacks all possession, since whatever constitutes it does not belong to it; (3) the experience does not possess a form that it imposes on its constituent elements; and (4) the experience is empty of substantially permanent being. Since all events are constituted by "non-self" because they are "empty" of "self-existence" (svabhāva), there are no permanent "things."

Cobb contends that there are remarkable affinities between these Buddhist notions and Whitehead's doctrine of the "consequent nature of God," as well as biblical portrayals of God and human selfhood. God's "consequent nature" names God's relation to temporal processes in their entirety. It is God's aim at the concrete realization of all possibilities in their proper season.[10] For Cobb, this means that God is "empty" of self insofar as "self" is understood as an essence that can be preserved by excluding "other" things and events.[11] It is at this juncture that he and other process theologians separate themselves from classical Christian theism. In his view, theology should reject notions of God as an unchanging substance as well as the immortality of the human soul—notions rooted in Greek philosophy—by reappropriating biblical, especially Pauline teachings. In other words, dialogue with Buddhism, mediated through Whiteheadian process philosophy, brings theological reflection into closer alignment with biblical tradition, given the fact that traditional Christian teaching of God as an unchanging substantial essence, as well as the doctrine of an immortal soul, are in harmony neither with biblical tradition nor the "structure" of Christian experience.

It is not only Christian tradition that can be creatively transformed through dialogue with Buddhism. Since Buddhism and Christianity are different "structures of existence," Buddhists will experience the process of creative transformation through dialogue with Christians differently. While the specific character of this process is up to Buddhists to decide for themselves, Cobb suggests that there are areas where Buddhists could learn from Christianity. For example, in Japanese Pure Land Buddhism (jōdo shinshū or "True Pure Land School"), Amida Buddha is ultimate reality personified as compassionate wisdom that brings all sentient beings into the Pure Land through his "other-power" without regard to a being's "self-power." Cobb suggests that dialogue with Pauline-Augustinian-Lutheran traditions of "justification by faith through grace alone" can deepen Buddhist understanding of this form of religious experience, thereby deepening the personal dimension of its own traditions. Here, the experience of "faith through grace" and the

10. Whitehead, Process and Reality, 31.
11. See Cobb and Griffin, Process Theology, 136–42.

experience of Amida Buddha's compassionate "other power" provide a common experiential entry point for Buddhist-Christian dialogue.[12] Furthermore, Buddhists can learn much from the Christian doctrine of the incarnation: in the life, death, and resurrection of a human being living two thousand years on the fringes of the Roman Empire, human beings encountered God incarnated within the rough and tumble of historical existence. For Christians, this means that the experience of faith and its doctrinal interpretations are historically contextualized.

Buddhists, particularly in Japan, are beginning to incorporate historical research into Buddhist thought. Yet Cobb claims that Jōdo Shinshū Buddhists have not yet worked through the problem of the relation of history to Buddhist faith and practice. In Cobb's words, Buddhists can "indeed find in Gautama himself and in the history of Buddhism much to support it. However, there is nothing about Buddhist self-understanding that leads to the necessity of finding the requisite history solely in India and East Asia."[13] Like Christianity, Buddhism intends universality and like Christianity, Buddhism too needs an inclusive view of all things. Today, such a view must include world history. World history includes the history of Israel and Jesus. Therefore, including the history that supports Christian claims about the graciousness of God into its own particular history supports, as it universalizes, Jōdo Shinshū claims of the universal compassionate wisdom that characterizes ultimate reality personified as Amida Buddha.

John B. Keenan

Perhaps the most radical attempt to reinterpret Christian theology through the categories of Buddhist thought is John P. Keenan's reading of Christian tradition through the lenses of Mahayana Buddhist philosophy, particularly the idealist metaphysics of Yogacāra ("Way of Yoga") philosophy and Mādhyamika ("Middle Way") epistemology, as a means of clarifying New Testament understandings of Christ.[14] Keenan sees his theological task as developing new forms of christological thought capable of expressing faith in ways relevant to post-modern experience of the relativity of all normative claims about reality. Accordingly, Keenan's theological construction of a "Mahayana Christology" focuses on demonstrating how the Christ that was incarnate in the historical

---

12. Cobb, *Beyond Dialogue*, 128–43.

13. Ibid., 139.

14. Keenan, *The Meaning of Christ*, Introduction.

Jesus is also the "heart of wisdom" attested to in the Gospel of John, the Synoptic Gospels, the Pauline Epistles, and the Epistle of James.[15]

By "heart of wisdom" Keenan means experiential apprehension of the structures of existence as interdependent, an apprehension he believes is at the core of both Buddhist and biblical traditions. A second goal of Keenan's Mahayana Christology is to regain contact with biblical meanings as a means of reinterpreting orthodox christological traditions in a manner spiritually relevant to a post-modern, post-Christian age characterized by religious pluralism.

The specifically Christian textual sources of Keenan's Mahayana theology lie in the wisdom traditions of the Hebrew Bible and Christian experience of Christ as the wisdom of God incarnate in the historical Jesus and all things and events in space-time (John 1:1–14). He believes that the Mahayana Buddhist name for this Wisdom is "Emptying" or *śūnyatā*, which in Buddhist tradition has no theistic connotations whatsoever. Nevertheless, Keenan asserts that what Mahayana philosophy describes as "wisdom," meaning the apprehension of the interdependence of all things and events as empty of independent and permanent self-existence or "own-being" (*svabhāva*), is philosophically and experientially similar to biblical teaching regarding Christ as the Wisdom through which God creates and sustains the universe. It is in this sense that Wisdom or the Logos is incarnated not only in Jesus, but also in all things and events in the universe at every moment of space-time. For this reason, it seems to Keenan, Buddhist teachings about interdependence and non-self clarify Christian experience of interdependence and the "emptiness" of all things and events of permanent "own-being."[16]

Another example of how Keenan applies Mahayana philosophy to the service of Christian theological reflection is his interpretation of how the historical Jesus incarnates the Logos. According to his Mahayana interpretation of the historical Jesus, Jesus—like all phenomenal things and events—is empty of any unchanging essence that might identify Jesus and serve as an unchanging definition of the historical Jesus as a "Jesus-self" that remains self-identical through time. This does not mean that we cannot form any notion of what Jesus was like, for the Gospel traditions and the writings of St. Paul point to a clearly identifiable human being. Yet the historical Jesus possesses no clearly identifiable selfhood beyond Jesus' dependently co-arising words and actions recorded in the biblical texts. There is no permanent selfhood for Jesus at all, since all things and events—including human

---

15. Ibid., 221–39. Also see Keenan, *The Gospel of Mark: A Mahayana Reading*, 3–43.

16. Keenan, *The Meaning of Christ*, 225–29.

beings—according to Mahayana philosophy *and* biblical tradition, are empty of permanent selfhood.

In place of seeking an understanding of Jesus as the Christ in terms of identifiable metaphysical essences, for example as was done in the Nicene and Chalcedonian Creeds, Keenan argues that Christian theology should shed all essentialist metaphysics by concentrating on the themes of emptying and non-self. Nowhere did Jesus as portrayed in the Gospels cling to permanent selfhood. The Gospel of John and the Synoptic Gospels, the Pauline Epistles, and the Epistle of James specifically identify Jesus with wisdom, meaning in its New Testament context, an immediate awareness of God as Father (Abba).[17] Matthew identifies receptivity to wisdom with a childlike disposition unspoiled by learning coupled with non-clinging to permanent selfhood (Matthew 18:1–10). Or, as understood through the lens of Mahayana Buddhist thought, the primary motif of the Gospels, the Pauline Epistles, and the Epistle of James is a call for conversion away from a "sign-clinging mind" that would equate faith with a single doctrinal position to a mind that is receptive of the Spirit and thereby aware of God as Abba, which Keenan believes is the heart of "Christian Wisdom." "Jesus disappears in the reality he proclaims. In Ch'an (Zen) Buddhist terms, he is a finger pointing at the moon."[18]

Hans Küng

Unlike Cobb and Keenan, Hans Küng's conceptual dialogue with Buddhism does not lead him to incorporate Buddhist doctrines into his theology as a means of creatively transforming Christian tradition. Küng's theological interpretation of Buddhism presupposes Vatican II's theology of religion. Specifically, he employs a comparative methodology in his theological engagement with Buddhist traditions, noting that post-Vatican II Catholicism has irrevocably committed itself to dialogue with the world's religions. Relying on scholarship in Buddhist studies as well as his personal participation in Buddhist-Christian dialogue, Küng's method is concerned with pointing out what he perceives are the similarities between Christian and Buddhist doctrines and practices, as well as the incommensurable differences. His theological goal is the clarification of differences in order to help Christians gain accurate comprehension of Christian faith while simultaneously helping Buddhists obtain clearer understanding of Christianity.

17 Ibid., chaps. 38–42

18. Ibid., 228.

The starting point of his conversation with Buddhism is his comparison of the historical Jesus and the historical Buddha, and the roles of Jesus and the Buddha play in Christian and Buddhist tradition. Küng first notes "a fundamental similarity not only in Jesus' and the Buddha's conduct, but also in their message": both were teachers whose authority lay in their experience of an ultimate reality; both had urgent messages, although the content of each differed, which demanded of people fundamental changes of attitude and conduct; neither intended to give philosophical explanations of the world nor did they aim to change existing legal and social structures; both worked from the assumption that the world is transient; both taught that all human beings are in need of redemption and transformation; both saw the root of humanity's unredeemed state in human egoism, self-seeking, and self-centeredness; and both taught ways of redemption.[19]

Yet in spite of the similarities Küng perceives between Jesus and the Buddha as historical figures in the history of religions, what he characterizes as "the smiling Buddha" and the "suffering Christ" reveal not only incommensurable difference between Christianity and Buddhism, but also several "tensions" inherent within Buddhism itself that Buddhists might address through conceptual dialogue with Christian thought. As Küng interprets the history of early Buddhism, after Gautama achieved his Awakening, he spent the next forty years of his life teaching and gathering an inner circle of disciples to form the first monastic community in the history of the world's religions. This monastic community (*samgha*) grew and was supported by a larger lay community of unordained men and women. The Buddha taught detachment from the rough-and-tumble of political and social existence, counseling his monks to seek Awakening by withdrawing into the practice of meditation, and his lay followers to live in society as nonviolently as possible in order to acquire positive karmic merit in the hope of achieving a better rebirth in a future life. The Buddha was quite successful in his lifetime, and he died peacefully after forty years of teaching and forming his monastic community.

Jesus was altogether different. His public life lasted at most for three years and ended in a violent death. His whole life, Küng argues, was a life of suffering without a trace of success in his lifetime. When he died, he was alone, deserted by even his closest disciples, the image of the sufferer pure and simple, which the earliest Christian community interpreted as an act of supreme self-sacrifice that demonstrated God's love for humanity. Jesus was not a teacher of monasticism, and demanded that his followers take up a life

19. Küng, *Christianity and the World Religions*, 322.

of social engagement with the forces of injustice and oppression in the world based on love for neighbors and compassion for the poor and the oppressed. Jesus was not a monk and he did not create a monastic community as the central path for his followers. Monasticism, although still practiced in several different forms of Christian tradition, is not central to Jesus' teaching of the kingdom of God nor is it central for Christian faith or a necessary means for salvation. Salvation is eternal life in the kingdom of God, into which all are welcome who follow Jesus' way of selfless love directed toward all. For Jesus the sufferer not only exudes compassion, but also demands it as the defining expression of the community that follows his way.

Gautama also knew suffering, which was his first Noble Truth: all existence is suffering (*duhkha*). The key to release from suffering, the Buddha taught, lies within human beings. Self-discipline in the practice of nonviolence toward any living thing and the practice of meditation are the sole requirements for the achievement of Awakening, the attainment of which leads to no further rebirth in the realm of samsaric suffering. Awakened ones, that is buddhas, are eventually "extinct," no longer involved in the cycles of rebirth that constitute existence. Accordingly, the Buddha is a paradigm, a model against which his followers are taught to test and measure their own progress toward Awakening. The emphasis of Buddhist practice is self-effort, not reliance on a power outside of one's self-efforts: in following the Buddha's example, one becomes *like* the Buddha. For Buddhists, the Buddha is the one who shows the way to Awakening.

But the historical Jesus as the Christ, for Christians, *is* the way. That is, Jesus *became* the way of salvation, meaning eternal life in the kingdom of God made manifest in his life, death, and resurrection. Salvation comes through trust in Jesus as the Christ expressed through active and loving social engagement with the world in the struggle to create a human community based on love and justice. The model of this community is the kingdom of God, partly realized in the community of faith called the church and completed in the future when God finally achieves God's intentions in creation. Thus salvation in Christian tradition and Awakening in Buddhist tradition are not identical concepts or experiences, even though Christians can learn much from the practice of meditation. Even so, Küng believes Buddhists indeed experience salvation through Christ's "extraordinary" working through the practice and traditions of faithful Buddhists, some of whom have attained Awakening. While Christians can and should be open to Buddhist experience and can learn much from Buddhist insights regarding interdependence, suffering and its causes, the ordinary way of salvation is through faith in Jesus as the Christ.

Winston L. King

King was an important historian of religions whose scholarship in this academic field became the foundation of his theological encounter with Buddhism. Drawing on years of academic engagement in Buddhist studies and his participation in Buddhist-Christian dialogue, his primary theological interest was the clarification of the purposes of genuine interreligious dialogue. For King, the essential purpose of dialogue was not "dialogical action," his designation for what Buddhists now call "social engagement," meaning humanistic cooperation among faith traditions in resolving social issues. Nor is dialogue the sharing of spiritual techniques in the practice of "interior dialogue." While recognizing the importance of both forms of interreligious encounter, the essential purpose of Buddhist-Christian dialogue, indeed of Christian dialogue with the world religions in general, is addressing the doctrinal "sticking points" between religious traditions. For King, Buddhist-Christian conceptual dialogue does not involve incorporating Buddhist concepts into Christian theological reflection because the moment one does so, one ceases to be Christian or Buddhist.[20]

Still, King believed that genuine interreligious dialogue requires that participants be committed to their own religious tradition while simultaneously remaining open to the possibility of conversion to the religious tradition of one's dialogical partner. Such a dialogue is more than mere friendship and toleration of differing points of view. Dialogue requires openness to deep change, which for King implied willingness to face one's own incompleteness. For this reason, he thought few persons ever seriously engage in interreligious dialogue. Therefore, since doctrinal issues are at the heart of interreligious dialogue, King pointed to three doctrinal issues that generate non-negotiable differences, meaning core teachings so necessary to both traditions that they are not open to challenge.[21]

First, King doubted that Christian theism would ever have much to contribute conceptually to most Buddhists, while Buddhist non-theistic teachings about ultimate reality will not have much conceptual appeal for Christians.

---

20. W. L. King, "Interreligious Dialogue." Also see W. L. King, *Buddhism and Christianity*, chap. 1.

21. W. L. King, "Interreligious Dialogue," 50–55.

Second, Christian and Buddhist conceptions of human selfhood are likewise incommensurable. Regarding the third area, "religiously inspired social action," King thought that Christian tradition is much more socially engaged in the struggle against human and environmental injustice than Buddhist tradition, and therefore Christians do not have much to learn from Buddhists. Thus he argued that because Christian faith and practice focus attention on the world in a way that is foreign to Buddhist teaching and practice—because of Buddhism's teaching that Awakening is experienced by means of meditation as a timeless moment that transcends the flux of historical space-time realities—Buddhists in dialogue with Christians might deepen their sense of history and help Buddhists become better prepared for social engagement.[22]

Seiichi Yagi, Masaaki Honda, and Lynn de Silva

A number of important East Asian and South Asian theologians have engaged in theological dialogue with Buddhism as a means of reinterpreting Christian faith through elements of the Buddhist worldviews of their cultures. Within the context of the Society for Buddhist-Christian Studies, the most important are Seiichi Yagi, Masaaki Honda, and Lynn Ade Silva. Honda and Yagi are Japanese theologians who live in a culture permeated with Buddhist images and ideals and whose theological reflections are in large measure a response to the creative presence of Buddhism in a culture in which Christian faith and practice are foreign. As do Cobb and Keenan, Yagi and Honda—though in different ways—intentionally expose their Christian experience to interpretation through the lenses of Buddhism, much as the church fathers and mothers filtered their Christian experience through the lenses of Hellenistic philosophy. Which is to say that both are committed Japanese Christians who focus on translating the deepest levels of faith through the categories of Buddhist thought and practice in an effort to integrate Christian tradition more coherently with cultural traditions that are non-Western.

Yagi is a biblical scholar who is known for using the techniques of literary and historical criticism to compare the religious consciousness of Paul with that of Shinran (the thirteenth-century "founder" of Jōdo Shinshū) and the consciousness of the historical Jesus with that of Zen masters. By specifying three kinds of religious experience—the communal, the individual, and the interpersonal—he develops an interpretation of Christian experience of the transcendent whereby the religious experience of Paul is correlated with

22. Ibid., 55.

Shinran, while Jesus' awareness and articulation of God parallels those of Zen statements in which there is neither a dualistic awareness nor a focus on concerns pertaining to the usual self. He concludes that the structures of Christian and Buddhist experience are similar, which, he argues, establishes a foundation for Asian theological reflection that transcends the usual categories of Western philosophy.[23]

Whereas Yagi uses biblical studies and comparative methodologies for theological reflection on Buddhism, Honda grounds his theology on his interpretation of foundational Christian doctrines, especially the doctrines of the two natures of Christ, the Trinity, and creation *ex nihilo*. Rejecting the epistemological assumptions of Greek philosophy and Cartesian epistemology, he rethinks these key Christian doctrines through the categories of the Japanese Zen Buddhist philosopher Kitaro Nishida, especially Nishida's "topological logic," or what Honda calls "the Buddhist logic of *soku*" or "not same, not different." He thus claims that the structure of the Buddhist and Christian "spiritual fact"—the simultaneously irreversible and reversible relation of the Dharma and God to the world—are identical. For this reason, in expressing the deepest awareness of God, the origins of the universe, and the self, Christian truth claims should be expressed in the awareness of *soku*, and therefore beyond the capacity of doctrines to completely capture or articulate. The result is a transformed vision of Christian theology, which remains committed to Christ, yet appropriates the insights of Buddhist experience and doctrine.[24]

Few Christian thinkers are in explicit dialogue with the Theravada (Elder's School) Buddhist tradition. Lynn de Silva, who worked in Sri Lanka, is an important exception. In similarity with Honda and Yagi, the question that guided his theological reflection is how Christian faith can be articulated in forms meaningful to South Asian Christians apart from Western cultural norms. Since Theravada Buddhism underlies the culture of not only Sri Lanka, but also all of South Asia—with the exception of Vietnam, where Mahayana forms of Buddhism predominate—de Silva interpreted Christian experience through the lenses of the Buddhist tradition of his culture. In so doing, he believed he was not falsifying Christian tradition. In his view, the importation Western cultural norms and thought forms as a means of inter-

23. See Yagi, "Paul and Shinran, Jesus and Zen"; and Swindler, *A Bridge to Buddhist-Christian Dialogue*, chaps. 1–4. Also see Yagi, "Buddhist-Christian Dialogue in Japan."

24. Honda, "The Encounter of Christianity with the Buddhist Logic of *Soku*."

preting Christian faith to South Asian Christians constitutes a falsification of Christian tradition for South Asians.

De Silva's engagement with Buddhism focused on the "problem of the self." According to him, the Buddhist doctrine of "non-self" (Pali *anatta*; Sanskrit *anātman*) enshrines an essential truth about human existence, which is in accord with not only contemporary science, but also the Hebrew Bible and the New Testament. While the idea of an immortal soul is an established belief for most Christians, it cannot be supported by biblical texts. Furthermore, biblical images of selfhood are corroborated by the Buddhist doctrine of non-self. It other words, the Buddhist doctrine of non-self reveals the meaning of selfhood in the biblical texts—meanings that are lost when biblical texts are read through the lenses of Greek philosophical notions about the soul. In the biblical tradition, the self is an interdependent psycho-physical unity of "soul" (*psychē*), "flesh" (*sarx*), and "spirit" (*pneuma*) that bears close resemblance to the Buddhist analysis of the self by means of the Five Skandhas or constituents of existence (form, feeling, perception, impulses, and consciousness). Consequently, Buddhist *and* biblical views of the self agree that there exists no immortal soul that remains self-identically permanent through time.

Not only does the Buddhist notion of non-self clarify biblical notions of selfhood, it also clarifies the doctrine of the resurrection. For if persons are constituted by non-self, the question remains: what continues after death? In contrast to the Buddhist doctrine of reincarnation, the biblical answer is the doctrine of resurrection. Resurrection does not mean the survival of an immortal soul or a reconstituted corpse. For if the doctrine of non-self corresponds to reality, transience and mortality are cosmic facts and death is the end of existence. There cannot be survival after death unless, and only if, God re-creates a new being. This, according to de Silva, is the truth of the biblical teaching of resurrection interpreted through the lenses of the doctrine of non-self. Resurrection is an act of God by which he creates what St. Paul called a "spiritual body." To explain the meaning of "spiritual body" de Silva employed a "replica theory," according to which at the moment of death, God creates an "exact psycho-physical replica of the deceased person." It is a new creation. But because it is a re-creation, the spiritual body is not identical with the self that existed in an earthly body. It is an exact psychophysical replica. The doctrine of the resurrection as a "replication" is, he believed, a way of meaningfully reconceiving "the hereafter while accepting the fact of *anātta*."[25]

25. de Silva, *The Problem of the Self in Buddhism and Christianity*, 7.

BUDDHIST CONCEPTUAL DIALOGUE WITH CHRISTIANITY

Like Christian tradition, Buddhism began as a missionary movement whose goal was to engage with non-Buddhists "for the welfare of the people, for the tranquility of the people, out of love for the people of the world" by means of converting non-Buddhists to Buddhism.[26] However, pluralist approaches to non-Buddhist religious traditions do not have much historical precedence in Buddhist history. This is not surprising since pluralism as a theological or philosophical interpretation of the fact of religious diversity is a specifically contemporary phenomenon. Still, Buddhist attitudes toward non-Buddhist traditions have ranged from exclusivism to acceptance of other religions as inferior, but pragmatically useful for gaining worldly benefits such as health and prosperity. Rarely have Buddhists acknowledged that Buddhism is equally conditioned and fallible as other religious traditions, or accepted non-Buddhist teachings and practices as having equal validity with those of Buddhism. In fact, most Buddhists engaged in conceptual dialogue with Christians argue that pluralism constitutes an inauthentic Buddhist response to religious diversity, so that a Buddhist form of the "pluralist hypothesis" seems not to have been an option in the history of Buddhism's encounter with non-Buddhists.

As I shall note more fully below, Buddhist responses to pre-modern and post-modern non-Buddhist religious traditions are filtered through certain key doctrines, such as the Mahayana doctrines of "emptying" (*śūnyatā*) and "two truth" (Sanskrit *Satya-dvaya*) epistemological theories. For example, there are numerous examples scattered throughout early Buddhists texts describing the Buddha's meeting with various representatives from different religious groups and giving a variety of religious responses to them. Some of these responses were quite critical. The Buddha was apparently critical of a number of Vedic Hindu practices, for example animal sacrifices and the caste system, because such practices and social systems foster violence. At other times he appears to have accepted, while subordinating, other religious practices, such as veneration of the gods. Often he accepted, but modified other practices such as worship of the six directions, the meaning of being a true Brahmin or "priest," and meditation traditions having their roots in Yoga. In East Asia, Buddhism always coexisted with Confucianism, Daoism, and Shinto with varying

---

26. *Vinaya, Mahavaga* I:10, from Nakamura, *Gotama Buddha*, 83; also cited by Chappell, "Buddhist Interreligious Dialogue," 5.

degrees of accommodation and assimilation.[27] Even in South Asian Theravada Buddhism, where Buddhism became, and remains, the dominant religious tradition, worship of the gods and honor to ancestors has not ceased among most practicing Buddhists.

Besides the rejection of some non-Buddhist religious traditions and practices, there are other examples of Buddhist views of non-Buddhists religious traditions that are also quite similar to those of first- and second-century Christianity. Buddhist responses to non-Buddhist religious traditions were sometimes inclusivist, sometimes exclusivist, sometimes highly negative, and often monological in structure. Doctrinally, non-Buddhist religions were sometimes depicted as not necessarily false, but rather inadequate, distracting, distorted, or evil. Ritual initiation into Buddhism by means of "taking the Precepts" usually meant explicitly vowing not to follow other religious teachers or to study other religious traditions.

But in the nineteenth century these patterns of Buddhist interaction with non-Buddhist religious traditions began to assume a more explicitly dialogical form as Buddhists became more acquainted with worldwide religious pluralism. Specifically, Buddhists became more interested in socially engaged dialogue than conceptual dialogue with non-Buddhist traditions in general and Christian tradition in particular. This is so because Buddhist tradition is hardwired to a specific worldview in a way other religious traditions are not. Change or delete any item from this worldview, Buddhism ceases to be Buddhism. All schools of Buddhism, in their own distinctive ways, are theoretical interpretations of this worldview.

Foundational to this worldview is the Buddha's teaching that all existence is implicated in suffering and impermanence (*duhkha* and *anitya*); that we cause suffering for ourselves and others by clinging (*tanha*) to permanence in an impermanent universe; that release from suffering is possible; that the Noble Eightfold Path is the ethical and meditative practice that leads to the cessation of suffering and the achievement of Awakening (Nirvana). Crucial to the Buddha's teaching about the structure of impermanent existence for not only all sentient beings, but also the entire universe, are the doctrines of interdependence (*pratīya-samutpāda*) and non-self (*anātman*). "Non-self" means that all things and events at every moment of space-time are constituted by the ceaselessly changing interrelationships things and events undergo from

27. This was particularly the case in Japanese Buddhism, where its "philosophy of assimilation" (*honji-suijaku*) had its origins in Chinese and Korean traditions of Buddhism imported to Japan. See Matsunaga and Matsunaga, *Foundation of Japanese Buddhism*.

moment to moment of their existence. There exists only interdependent relationships undergoing ceaseless change and becoming. Or in more Buddhist language, all things and events at every moment of space-time are constituted by the process of *pratīya-samutpāda* or "interdependent co-arising."

These doctrines are presupposed in every aspect of Buddhist teaching and practice even as they are nuanced differently in the various schools of Buddhism. Applied to human beings, for example, non-self means that we are not embodiments of an unchanging self-entity that remains self-identical through time. All Buddhist teachings are firm in their rejection of permanent selfhood. What we "are" is a system of interdependent relationships— physical, psychological, historical, sociological, cultural, spiritual—that, in interdependence with everything else undergoing change and becoming in the universe, continuously create "who" we are from moment to moment in our lifetimes. We are not permanent selves that *have* these interdependent relationships; we *are* these interdependent relationships we undergo. Since these relationships are not permanent, neither we nor anything else in the universe is permanent.

In some ways, Buddhism is more worldview-specific than, say, Christian tradition, even though the Christian worldview is monotheistic. As noted above, delete any of the foundational doctrines from Buddhism's worldview, Buddhism ceases to be Buddhist, just as deleting monotheism from Christianity's worldview makes Christianity unchristian. Even so, Buddhism is worldview-specific in a way that Christianity is not. A Christian can be a Marxist, a NeoPlatonist, a communist, a Kantian, a Whiteheadian, a Hegelian, a Thomist, a death-of-God theologian, or even "a Buddhist, too," according to John Cobb, provided one is careful to specify what this means.[28] To this date, no Buddhist has claimed "a Buddhist can be a Christian, too."

I do not mean by these observations that Buddhist tradition is inferior to Christian tradition. Nor do I mean to imply that either Buddhism or Christianity are forms of religious imperialism, which is not to say that there have not existed Buddhist and Christian forms of religious imperialism. My intention is descriptive: I am suggesting that a difference exists between the structure of Buddhist existence and the structure of Christian existence which makes it difficult for Buddhists to engage in conceptual dialogue with non-Buddhists from a pluralist perspective. Again, this is not to say that no Buddhists have conceptually engaged with Christianity. In fact it can be

28. See Cobb, "Can a Buddhist Be a Christian, Too?"

argued that the first contemporary Buddhist-Christian conceptual dialogue began in Japan in 1957.

The Kyoto School

The Buddhist origins of this dialogue have their roots in the early twentieth century, beginning with Nishida Kitaro (1879–1945). Under Nishida's leadership, the philosophy department at Kyoto University began a conceptual dialogue with Western culture, particularly Christian tradition, by offering a series of critical analyses based on Buddhist ideals. Several disciples of Nishida—Tanabe Hajime (1885–1962), Hisamatsu Shin'ichi (1899–1980), Nishitani Keiji (1900–1990), and Masao Abe (1915–2006)—formed what is known as the Kyoto School. The Buddhist tradition espoused by the Kyoto School was Zen Buddhism coupled with an interest in Western Continental philosophy, particularly Kantian idealism. While utilizing Western philosophical traditions, the Kyoto School also employed Buddhist philosophy, particularly Mādhyamika epistemology and Zen traditions of meditation, to seek the absolute truth, identified as (*śūnyatā*) or "Emptying," that is beyond all rational limits. Perhaps the clearest expression of the Kyoto School's philosophical method and intention is Hisamatsu's *Tōyo-teki Mu* or *Oriental Nothingness*, written in 1939.

Following World War II, Hisamatsu sent his student Abe Masao to Union Theological Seminary for two years to study Christianity under Paul Tillich and Reinhold Niebuhr. Then, in 1957, Hisamatsu himself went to Harvard for the fall semester and engaged Tillich in several meetings that mark the beginning of modern Buddhist-Christian conceptual dialogue. These remarkable dialogues were later published in three issues of *The Eastern Buddhist*, a journal started by D. T. Suzuki.[29] Hisamatsu and Tillich were important thinkers in their traditions, and they were eager to engage in dialogue with one another. Hisamatsu expressed to Tillich that he wished to learn about themes in Tillich's theology such as "God beyond God" and Tillich's understanding of the nature of humanity.[30] Hisamatsu's focus in this concern was what Zen refers to as the "Formless Self" experienced at the moment of Awakening. Thus rather than focusing on what was doctrinally unique in Buddhist and Christian teaching, Hisamatsu wanted to push his conversation with Tillich beyond discursive traditions to seek what is experientially

29. De Martino, trans., "Dialogues East and West," 3 parts.
30. Ibid., (1972) 107.

common to human existence as such. This remains the primary focus of the Kyoto School's conceptual dialogue with Christian tradition. Tillich insisted, however, that except for Christ, human beings located in space-time can only partially realize the infinite reality (which he named "God"), while Hisamatsu argued that everyone could do provided they rejected all finite distinctions at the level of the formless self. This claim led Hisamatsu and his student Abe Masao to the doctrine of the "reversibility" of the ultimate and the finite, of the Buddha Nature and other things, of past and future. This doctrine has since become a point of disagreement not only with Christian and Jews, but also with most other Buddhists.[31]

Abe's interpretation of "reversibility" and his and Hisamatsu's interpretation of Emptying led to conclusions similar to that of Rahner's notion of "anonymous Christianity." Both of these teachers transformed Nagarjuna's epistemological use of Emptying into a metaphysically absolute ultimate reality which is the ground of all religious experience, but which is manifested most clearly in Buddhist, particularly Zen, teachings and practices. Accordingly, Christians who realize the experiential depth of their particular teachings partially glimpse Emptying even if they think they are experiencing God. This implies that Christians are "anonymous Buddhists," although neither Hisamatsu nor Abe explicitly used this terminology. Still, Hisamatsu's conceptual dialogue with Christianity and Abe's conceptual dialogue with Christianity and Judaism represent contemporary forms of Buddhism inclusivism.

Bihikkhu Buddhadasa

An eminent Thai Buddhist, Bihikkhu Buddhadasa (1906–1993), further refined Buddhist conceptual dialogue with Christianity with his "two languages theory": (1) dharma language and (2) conventional language. He interpreted the teachings of varying religious traditions, including Buddhist teachings, as "conventional language" while "dharma language" refers to language that expresses Awakening, which is only achieved through the practice of meditation. So while the conceptual differences between religious traditions are real, all religions are united in the higher truth concerning reality, to which

---

31. See the interchange between Abe and Christian and Jewish dialogue partners in Cobb and Ives, eds., *The Emptying God*; and Ives, ed., *Divine Emptiness and Historical Fullness*.

Buddhists and non-Buddhist mystics refer to in the paradoxes of "dharma language," so that all conventional linguistic distinctions melt away.

Furthermore, Buddhadasa argued that there exists a further level of religious experience in which religion itself disappears. He illustrated his theory of three levels of religion with the example of water. First, there are many kinds of water: rain water, tap water, sewer water, river water, which ordinary persons can use and distinguish, which illustrates what he meant by "conventional language." But at another level, when for example pollutants are removed, these conventional types of water turn out to be one substance, which illustrates what he meant by "dharma language." Finally, there is a third level of perception in which water disappears as it is divided into hydrogen and oxygen. So based on this analogy, Buddhsdasa concluded that there exist three levels of perception, each with its proper language: conventional distinctions, shared essence, and voidness.

Buddhadasa's approach to non-Buddhist traditions is similar to that of the Kyoto School, as illustrated in this chapter by Abe Masao. Linguistically structured conventional or relative truth points to, but does not capture, the absolute truth of Awakening that is beyond all language and form. Here, Empting is the absolute truth, underlying all valid religious teachings and practices, that is most fully experienced at the moment of Awakening through Buddhist meditative practices. Consequently, the conceptual dialogue of Buddhist teachers like Hisamatsu, Abe, and Buddhadasa with non-Buddhists is inclusivist in nature. In their own distinctive ways, each affirmed that other religious traditions and practices, including Buddhist doctrines, partially express truth more fully encountered in the achievement of Awakening by means of Buddhist meditative practices. This inclusivist viewpoint is also ingredient in the Dalai Lama's philosophy of religious pluralism: different religious traditions share a common goal that each seeks in their own distinctive ways. Specifically, he asserts that all religious traditions, in spite of conceptual differences, have similar objectives: the improvement of human existence and compassion for other life forms with which we share this planet, respect for others, and sharing other peoples' suffering while working to relieve suffering. At this level, which Buddhists call "social engagement," every religious tradition, in varying ways, share the same "secondary" viewpoints.[32]

---

32. Tenzin [His Holiness the XIV Dalai Lama], *Kindness, Clarity, and Insight*, 46.

SUMMARY OBSERVATIONS

Christian interest in conceptual dialogue with Buddhism—and other religious traditions—is a reflection of the monotheistic and christological structure of Christian existence. Christian existence starts with the incarnation. Two thousand years ago the first Jewish Christians believed they had experienced God in the life, death, and resurrection of the historical Jesus. The nature of this encounter was experientially clear to the first Christians. But interpreting what their experience implied about the character of God, the structure of community, how Christians should relate to the state, the Christian community's relation to Judaism and the Hellenistic religious traditions surrounding both Christianity and Judaism, and what the resurrection might imply about the possibility of a future beyond death, were matters that required the rational interpretation of experiential events that is called "theology." Theological reflection thus became a pillar of Christian faith and practice, which does not mean that other forms of practice such as social activism and contemplative practices are not important elements of Christianity's structure of existence. But while there is much theological agreement among Christians about the meaning of what the earliest Christians experienced in their encounter with the historical Jesus, there is also much theological disagreement. Nevertheless, theological reflection as "faith seeking understanding" of Christian experience is the center of Christian self-understanding. It has been so for two thousand years.

Accordingly, encounter with non-Christians has always been an important focus of Christian practice. Whenever encounter with non-Christians was dialogical, the primary form of dialogue was conceptual. When conceptual engagement with non-Christians focused on conceptual differences, the resulting theologies were exclusivist and the encounter was transformed into a conceptual monologue employed for the purpose of converting non-Christians to Christianity. When conceptual dialogue with non-Christians lead to appropriating non-Christian teachings and practices into Christian thought, the resulting theology of religions tended to be inclusivist. These patterns remain typical of contemporary liberal Christian conceptual engagement with Buddhism. But Christian pluralist theologies of religion are a rather new phenomenon and represent a minority theological viewpoint. Exclusivist, inclusivist, and pluralist engagement with Buddhism as well as other religious traditions have been primarily conceptual for most Christins.

Conceptual dialogue with Christianity is not a primary focus of Buddhist interest, which is not to say that conceptual engagement with Christian tradition has not occurred. While Buddhists have exerted much energy in achieving doctrinal clarity of the meaning of Buddhism's worldview, the primary emphasis of Buddhist practice is achieving release from suffering engendered by the achievement of Awakening—an experience that is only engendered by the disciplined practice of meditation. Conceptual disciplines like philosophy or doctrinal formulation play a supportive and secondary role to meditative practice. That is, the philosophical complexities of Buddhist doctrinal traditions are held to be secondary pointers that have the purpose of guiding the practice of meditation. Or in Buddhist language, they are "skill-ful devises" (Sanskrit *upāya*). Consequently, Buddhist doctrines are secondary constructs that point the way to Awakening, but only if the mediator does not cling to them. Clinging to a doctrinal construct or a philosophical teaching only increases suffering, for the reality experienced at the moment of Awakening transcends all conceptual pointers, including Buddhist pointers.

Consequently, most Buddhist dialogue with Christianity focuses on issues of social engagement. How Buddhists might act in partnership with Christians and non-Christians to overcome social, economic, and environmental injustice is the topic of chapter 4. But first, it is necessary to review important elements of Buddhist conceptual dialogue with the natural sciences because of its implications for both conceptual and socially engaged Buddhist-Christian dialogue, which is the topic of the next chapter.

3

Conceptual Dialogue with
the Natural Sciences

The natural sciences provide a continual stream of remarkable insights into the nature of physical reality across a wide range of domains. In the process, the natural sciences inspire wonder and, for most scientists and many faithful participants throughout the world's religious traditions, great reverence. It has been so since the sixteenth century. The sciences have changed both our world and our worldviews, and, in the process, our understanding of ourselves. This fact is the source of the many conceptual challenges the sciences pose for all religious traditions and systems of practice. As the pace of scientific discovery and innovation continues to increase exponentially, there arises an urgent cultural and religious need to reflect critically on these challenges by means of a constructive conceptual dialogue involving the world's religious traditions, including, of course, Buddhism and Christianity. One of the greatest challenges to this dialogue is the compartmentalization of knowledge as currently institutionalized in modern universities. Interreligious dialogue with the natural sciences requires an integrative dialogue among all the sciences, humanities, and the world's religious traditions.

The thesis of this chapter is that including the natural sciences as a third partner in contemporary Buddhist-Christian conceptual dialogue will engender new processes of creative transformation in both Buddhist and Christian traditions, and possibly in the sciences. So far, such a "trilogue" has not occurred. Yet the purpose of any dialogue is mutual creative transformation. For that transformation to occur within a Buddhist-Christian-science trilogue, the complex details of each of the natural sciences and Buddhist and Christian traditions need to be understood. Of course, conflicting views regarding the nature of reality need to be honestly recognized. But it must also be recognized that often, upon closer critical reflection, what seem like contradictions may turn out to be complementary ways of understanding reality. Ultimately, no truths can be contradictory if they are really true, provided we do not lock ourselves into a particular intellectual discipline or religious perspective, which only serves to confuse ideology with truth. Furthermore, Buddhist-Christian-science dialogue should not be limited to professional academics or religious leaders, but widened to include persons sitting in pews in churches and synagogues or on meditation cushions or prayer rugs in temples or mosques, as well as persons reading the Tuesday Science Section of the *New York Times*.

Exactly how an integrative Buddhist-Christian conceptual dialogue with the natural sciences should be structured remains an open question. But there exist Buddhist and Christian precedents.[1] What follows is a brief summary of these precedents that will focus on cosmology, evolutionary biology, and the neurosciences. What is obvious in these precedents is that Buddhists and Christians have greatly profited from their encounters with these scientific domains. But dialogue is a two-way conversation. Consequently, the final section of this chapter will focus on how the natural sciences might be creatively transformed through conceptual dialogue with Buddhist and Christian tradition.

COSMOLOGY

Since Christian monotheism and Buddhist non-theism appear, at first glance, incommensurable, reflection on the current scientific origin narrative that both Christians and Buddhists now share will serve as a means of highlighting the general structure of both tradition's conceptual encounter with the natural sciences. According to this narrative, some fourteen billion years ago the physical contents of the universe were together in an initial singularity, meaning a region of infinite curvature and energy density at which the known laws of physics break down (t=o).[2] There was a Big Bang. The history of the cosmos began approximately three minutes after this event, when protons and neutrons were combining to form nuclei. Five hundred thousand years

1. For a more detailed account of these precedents, see Ingram, *Buddhist-Christian Dialogue in an Age of Science.*

2. See Halliwell, "Quantum Cosmology and the Creation of the Universe."

later, atoms were coming into existence. One billion years from t=0, galaxies and stars were being formed, followed by planets at ten billion years. After another two billion years, microscopic forms of life were beginning to appear on our planet.

The farther back we go beyond three minutes, the more tentative this cosmological narrative becomes because theory must confront states of matter and energy increasingly farther from anything physicists can experimentally duplicate in the laboratory.[3] Protons and neutrons form from their constituent quarks at 10^{-4} seconds (a ten-thousandth of a second from t=0), when temperature had cooled to 10^{-12} (a trillionth of a degree). This sea of hot quarks would have formed at about 10^{-10} seconds from an even smaller and hotter fireball. According to the inflationary theories proposed by Alan Guth and Andrae Linde, the universe underwent a very rapid expansion at about 10^{-35} seconds due to the tremendous energy released in the breaking of symmetry when the strong force separated from the other forces.[4] Before 10^{-35} seconds, temperatures would have been so hot that all the forces except gravity were of comparable strength. Physicists have almost no idea about events before $t=10^{-45}$ seconds (Plank time), when the temperature was about 10^{-32} degrees, and the universe was about the size of an atom with an incredible density of 10^{96} times that of water.

In light of this origin narrative, it seems reasonable to ask what caused the Big Bang. There are currently no universally accepted scientific answers to this question. But the Christian answer is that God created the universe. But there is a problem with the Christian doctrine of creation that seems, at first glance, to point in the direction of Buddhist non-theism. The problem is that cosmologists claim that the Big Bang marked not only beginning of the universe, but also the beginning of time.[5] Time did not exist prior to the Big Bang, so there could have been no cause of the Big Bang. "What place then for a creator?" asks Stephen Hawking in *A Brief History of Time*, to which one might add, "or divine agency in the continuing processes of nature?"

The Buddhist answer to Hawking's question is that there is no place for a creator or divine agency. Non-theism has always been the center of the Buddhist worldview so that Buddhists like Geoffrey Redmond argue that contemporary cosmology readily harmonizes with Buddhism since Buddhism's cosmology can be construed as a metaphor without "weakening the Buddhist

3. See Weinberg, *The First Three Minutes*.

4. Guth and Steinhard, "The Inflationary Universe."

5. Hawking, *A Brief History of Time*, 141.

edifice." Furthermore, Redmond asserts that cosmology never had the centrality that creation has in Christian and Jewish tradition. "Buddhism never committed itself to a particular ontology," he writes, "which could be contradicted by modern psychological or anthropological conceptions of such beliefs as metaphorical or archetypal."[6] For this reason "Buddhism is closer to science" than Christian tradition "in the way it seeks truth."[7]

Clearly, the challenge of Big Bang cosmology to the Christian doctrine of creation is crystal clear. One way theologians have responded is by reflecting on the relation between space and time in the scientific origin narrative. According to this narrative, the Big Bang was an unusual explosion because it did not take place at a particular location in space. This means there existed no space outside the Big Bang. A common analogy to imagine this conclusion is a rubber balloon onto which are glued a number of coins. The coins represent galaxies. As air is pumped into the balloon, it expands. Suppose a fly was to land on one of the coins, what would it see? All the other coins moving away from it, which is, of course, the observed motion of the galaxies relative to scientists studying them from the Earth.

Astronomers currently think the motion of the galaxies is due to the space between galaxies expanding, rather than the galaxies moving through space. In other words, the galaxies are being carried outward from the singularity of the Big Bang on a tide of expanding space, just as coins glued to a balloon are carried apart by its rubber surface as the balloon expands. Furthermore, just as there is no empty stretch of rubber surface outside the region where the coins are clued, so there is no empty three-dimensional space outside where galaxies are to be found. It is this interpretation of the recession of the galaxies that leads cosmologists to conclude that all space that now exists was squashed to an infinitesimal singularity at the Big Bang. Space began as nothing and has continued to expand ever since.

There is an even more extraordinary element of this cosmology. According to Einstein's theory of general relativity, space and time are welded together as a four-dimensional continuum called "space-time." One cannot have space without time or time without space. In Buddhist language, they are "co-originated," meaning interdependent. This being so, the Big Bang marked not only the coming into existence of space, but also the existence of time. This means that as there is no space before the Big Bang, there is also no time before the Big Bang.

6. Redmond, "Comparing Science and Buddhism," 106.
7. Ibid., 111.

It is this aspect of contemporary scientific cosmology that many Buddhists believe gets rid of the sort of creator God that most people have in mind when they think of the Genesis creation story: a God who first exists alone and then at some point in time decides to create the universe. God says some words, there is a Big Bang, and creation begins. Indeed if the word "God" refers to this sort of entity, Buddhist non-theism seems more closely allied with current scientific cosmology than Christian monotheism.

Much depends, however, on the meaning of the word "God." Consider the following quotation from St. Augustine: "It is idle to look for time before creation, as if time can be found before time. If there were no motion of either a spiritual or corporal creature by which the future, moving through the present, would succeed the past, there would be no time at all. We should therefore say that time began with creation, rather than creation began with time."[8] That is, for God, there is neither before nor after; God simply is in a motionless eternity. Time and space are part of creation. Before creation, there is neither time nor space, and therefore, literally "nothing."[9] Deeply influenced by Platonic ideas, Augustine could write as early as his *Confessions*: "It is not in time that you [God] precede all times; all your 'years' subsist in simultaneity, because they do not change; your 'years' are 'one day' and your today is eternity.[10]

So, Augustine wrote, we know time exists because things change—in Buddhist language, all things change because all things are impermanent. If nothing changed, if nothing "moved" in Augustine's language, we could not distinguish one point in time from another and there would be no way of determining to what the word "time" refers. Accordingly, if there were no objects that change, that is, "move," there would be no objects at all. "Time" would be a meaningless category. Furthermore, if there is no time, there is no space (ether) through which objects move or occupy. In other words, no moving objects, no time; no time, no space.[11]

---

8. Augustine *De Civitate Dei* (*The City of God*) XII:15, cited by Stannard, "Where in the World Is God?" 13.

9. See Gilson, *The Christian Philosophy of Saint Augustine*, 190–91.

10. Augustine *Confessiones* XI; *Confessions*, 230.

11. *De Civitate Dei* XII:15: "For where there is no creature whose changing movements admits to succession, there cannot be time at all." So also XI:6: "time does not exist without some movement and transition." Also see Jordan, "Time and Contingency in St. Augustine"; and Lacy, "Empiricism and Augustine's Problem About Time."

Consequently, Augustine's theology of creation distinguished between ontological and historical origination, and he concluded that time and space are as much a property of the universe as anything else and it makes no sense to think of God predating the creation of the universe. Yet none of this had an adverse affect on Augustine's theology because he noted that there is an important distinction between the words "creation" and "origin." While in everyday conversations, we might use these words interchangeably, in Christian theological discourse since Augustine, each word has its own distinctive meaning. For example, if one has in mind a question like "How did the universe begin?" one is asking a question about historical "origins." Questions on origins are empirical matters for scientists to decide, their current research pointing to Big Bang cosmology. However, the question of the universe's "creation" is a theological issue.

Here is the theological argument: the doctrine of creation poses ontological issues that are quite different from those engendered by the universe's historical origins. In Christian teaching, creation has as much to do with the present instant of time as any other instant of time. Why is there something and not nothing? Why are we here? To whom or to what do we owe our existence? What keeps us in existence? Christian theological reflection on creation concerns the underlying ground of all things and events in space-time—past, present, and future. But the question of the universe's origins has to do with what started the physical processes that ended up as the universe.

The point of the forgoing discussion is to show that Buddhists see questions about the universe's ontological or historical origins as posing no significant challenges to Buddhist thought and practice. In fact, contemporary Buddhist writers tend to dismiss such questions as meaningless. In Buddhist cosmology, the universe is portrayed as an eternally changing system of interdependent interrelationships without beginning or end. Contemporary Western Buddhists especially think we should simply accept the universe as a brute fact and ask what, if anything, is gained by affirming that God created it. For Buddhists, the Christian doctrine of creation not only raises the question of who created God, it also implies that any notion of divine creation encourages clinging (*taṇhā*) to an imagined permanent sacred reality. The karmic result of such clinging to imagined permanent realities can only be suffering (*duhkha*).[12]

From a Christian perspective, however, standard Buddhist criticisms of Christian notions of creation usually misinterpret how Christian theology

12. See Taniguchi, "Modern Science and Early Buddhist Ethics."

uses the word "God." For example, Paul Tillich appropriated Augustine's no-tions of time when he wrote that God is not an existent object or "being."[13] In other words, one cannot say "God exists" in the same way that one can say "apples exist," or for that matter, "the universe exists." The point of the Christian doctrine of creation is that God is the source of all existence. "God" is the name Christians (and Jews and Muslims) give to whatever is responsible for the existence of all space-time things and events, including human beings. Most Buddhist interpretations of the Christian doctrine of creation, however, mistakenly assume that Christians affirm God as an object confined within the limits of space and time or that God can only exist in time. Certainly, one hears such theological talk among some evangelical and fundamentalist Christians. But the mainline teaching is that while we experience God in time and space, God is not confined by time and space.

If it is true that none of the conceptual challenges confronting the themes of traditional Christian theism—God as creator, both "in the be-ginning" and continually in the present—seemingly pose any challenge to Buddhism's non-theistic worldview, how can Buddhist faith and practice be creatively transformed through conceptual dialogue with Christian theology mediated by the sciences as a third party? Reflection on this question will require a brief description of standard Buddhist responses to the sciences.

For the most part, Buddhists have to this date stressed environmental ethics and psychology in their conversations with the natural sciences, which will be summarized in the following section.[14] This assertion does not im-ply that Buddhists have paid no attention to physics and biology. But as in Christian theology, the focus of Buddhist interest in the natural sciences stresses those areas where traditional Buddhist teachings might be supported by current scientific views of physical reality. In general, Buddhists interpret the natural sciences as a support for the doctrine of interdependence (*pratītya-samuptāda*), which teaches that everything and event at every moment of space-time is co-created and constituted by the interdependently interpen-etrating nexus of relationships it undergoes from moment to moment of its existence. Thus Buddhist interest in ecology is closely linked to the Buddhist doctrine of dependent co-origination, as are Buddhist teachings about non-self

13. Tillich, *Systematic Theology*, vol. 1, 235–92.

14. See, for example, Tucker and Williams, eds., *Buddhism and Ecology*; and three essays in Callicott and Ames, eds., *Nature in Asian Traditions of Thought*: Cook, "The Jeweled Net of Indra"; Inada, "Environmental Problems"; and Kaluphana, "Toward a Middle Path of Survival."

(*anatta, anātman*). Furthermore, the practice of meditation has led Buddhists to contemporary psychology and the neurosciences as a means of translating its traditional doctrines of suffering and its causes (*duhkha* and *taṇhā*), the meaning of "liberation" (*nirvāṇa*), and the practice of meditation into a more contemporary contexts.

B. Alan Wallace, who writes about the relation between scientific theory and reality through the lense of Tibetan Buddhist tradition, will serve to illustrate both a Buddhist critique of physics and biology and Buddhist interest in psychology. In contrast to Ian Barbour, Wallace is highly critical of the principle of critical realism in that he thinks that scientific theories do not have ontological correspondence to physical realities.[15] Barbour's "independence model" [16] best describes Wallace's thesis about the relation between science and Buddhism, since according to Wallace, "while the sciences give us objective knowledge about physical processes, the sciences do not give us knowledge of an objective world." [17] This means that the function of scientific theories is to make natural events intelligible for the purpose of developing technology that improves the quality of life for "all sentient beings." In other words, Wallace's approach to the sciences is instrumentalist: scientific conclusions about physical processes are pragmatically true because they lead to practical technological applications that improve the quality of life for all sentient beings.

Wallace's interpretation of the natural sciences is based on his appropriation of the "two-truths" epistemology that originated with the second-century Indian Buddhist logician Nagarjuna.[18] As pragmatic truths about the physical world, scientific truths are secondary truths that in themselves shed little light on the nature of reality. Absolute truth, however, is metaphysical and is named by Wallace in particular, and Nagarjuna in general, "Emptying" (śūnyatā); "Emptying" is the Absolute Truth to which Buddhas awaken through the practice of meditation. Therefore, Wallace concludes, "We err if we expect the natural sciences to solve issues of a metaphysical or religious

---

15. Wallace, *Choosing Reality*, chap. 11.

16. The independence model asserts that science and theology are independently autonomous enterprises. Each should keep off the other's turf; each should tend to its own specific affairs and not meddle in the concerns of the other. See Barbour, *Religion and Science*, 84–90.

17. Wallace, *Choosing Reality*, 14.

18. For an interpretation and translation of Nagarjuna's writings, see Streng, *Emptiness*.

nature, for it was never designed to probe such questions."[19] Furthermore, as secondary truths, the primary weakness of physics and the biological sciences is that "neither disciplines the mind and mental experience,"[20] a conclusion most working scientists reject.

Jeffrey Redmond notes that Buddhism first encountered Western science as part of its experience with sixteenth-century colonialism in South and East Asia. In this encounter, Buddhists do not appear to have felt the need to oppose Western science. Nor did the sciences challenge the fundamentals of Buddhism's worldview and doctrines in the way it challenged Christian theology. According to Redmond, this is because Buddhism is not committed to the pre-scientific ideas associated with it since Buddhism's traditional cosmology was never its essential core. Therefore, Buddhism was, and still is, less threatened by science than other world religions. Like Wallace, Redmond thinks Buddhism and the sciences are independent enterprises.[21]

Victor Mansfield takes Redmond's conclusions farther. He argues that similarities between Madhyamika philosophy and modern physics in their understanding of time is evidence that Buddhism is particularly compatible with the natural sciences, especially in the area of psychology.[22] But compatibility with the natural sciences does not imply that Buddhism is "scientific." Both Redmond and Mansfield, as well as most Buddhists, think that asserting that Buddhism is "scientific" is a distortion of Buddhism and science. So while science is no threat to Buddhist teachings and practice (because they are independent enterprises), Buddhism has resources that can fill in the gaps of Western science relative to analyzing subjective mental and emotional experiences that can help the psychological sciences overcome their Cartesian emphasis on objectivity, and thereby develop coherent theories of cognition. In other words, through dialogue with Buddhism science is more apt to be creatively transformed than is Buddhism because of Buddhism's "strong empirical foundations" and the "deconstructive traditions of Nagarjuna's Madhyamika ("Middle Way") dialectics," which Mansfield believes overcome the "objectivist weakness" he perceives in Western physics and biology.[23]

19. Ibid., 9.

20. Ibid.

21. Redmond, "Introduction." Also see Redmond, "Comparing Science and Buddhism."

22. Mansfield, "Time in Madhyamika Buddhism and Modern Physics."

23. Ibid., 65–67.

Finally, writing from a Theravada Buddhist perspective, Shoyo Taniguchi asserts that Buddhism is scientific in a way other religions are not. She scrutinizes the Pali Canon and early Buddhist philosophy and pushes the interdependence model as far as it can probably go. She concludes that early Theravada Buddhism employs empirical and experimental methods equivalent to those of modern science and is therefore a "scientific" religion, meaning that Buddhist doctrines harmonize with current scientific models of physical reality in a way other religions do not.[24] For this reason she concludes that Buddhism is "superior to other religions," particularly Judaism, Christianity, and Islam because, in her view, physics and evolutionary biology leave no room for a creator deity.

It is clear that Redmond, Mansfield, and Taniguhi do not experience or interpret the natural sciences—particularly Big Bang cosmology—as a challenge to Buddhist doctrine and practice. The distinct impression that contemporary Buddhist writing on the natural sciences seems to give is that the structure of Buddhist tradition remains untouched by none of the sciences, either positively or negatively.

EVOLUTIONARY BIOLOGY: TWO CHRISTIAN RESPONSES

The great discovery of Charles Darwin is that the adaptations and diversity of living organisms can be explained as an orderly natural process of change governed by natural laws organizing matter in motion without reference to religious myths about God. But Darwin faced a real problem when he wrote *Origin of Species*. A version of the classical argument by design by William Paley was almost universally held by the intellectuals of Darwin's day, including theologians and naturalists. Darwin himself had read Paley's book *Natural Theology* as a university student and found it much to his liking, but later changed his mind. Paley possessed extensive and accurate biological knowledge, as detailed and precise as possible in the mid-nineteenth century. His book is a sustained "argument by design" that claims that the living world supplies compelling evidence that it was created by an omnipotent and omniscient creator. The core of Paley's argument was his claim that "there cannot be a design without a designer; contrivance without contriver; order without choice; means unsuitable to an end, and executing their office in accomplishing that end, without the end ever having been contemplated."[25] Again and

24. Taniguchi, "Modern Science and Early Buddhist Ethics."

25. William Paley, *Natural Theology*; quoted by Ayala, *Evolutionary and Molecular Biology*, 25.

again, Paley drew the conclusion that only an omnipotent and omniscient deity could account for the astonishing complexity and structural order of biological processes. Thus, just as someone finding a watch on a beach can draw the certain conclusion that a watchmaker exists, so the complex structure of the human eye can only be explained by the existence of a deity who designed it.

Darwin accepted the notion that organisms are "designed," but not by a creator. He argued that inherited adaptive variations, adaptations useful in the survival of species in their particular environments, are most likely to appear in organisms. When these adaptations occur, the odds for an organism's survival increases over those organisms in the same species that do not have these adaptations. Those who do survive reproductively pass on their adaptive variations to future generations because they are the most reproductively successful, while the members of a species that have not adapted die off. Darwin's term for the preservation of favorable variations and the rejection of unfavorable variations was "natural selection." If enough favorable adaptations are passed on reproductively to new generations over time, the original species will become extinct and be replaced by a new species suitable for survival in its particular environment. In short, evolution is a process of natural selection that "designs" all organisms relative to their environments.

But exactly how natural selection occurs is not clear in Darwin's original theory of evolution. It was the rediscovery in 1900 of Gregory Mendel's theory of hereditary that brought genetics into evolutionary theory as a means of explaining how natural selection actually takes place. Today evolutionary theory is formulated in genetic and statistical terms as differential reproduction, a form of evolutionary theory often referred to as "neo-Darwinism" by nonscientists, even though working scientists seldom employ this term. According to the majority contemporary interpretation, natural selection causes some genes and genetic combinations to have higher probabilities of being transmitted than their alternatives. These genetic units will become more common in subsequent generations as their alternatives become less common. In other words, natural selection over time is a statistical bias in the relative rate of reproduction of alternative genes. In this way natural selection acts like a filter that eliminates harmful genetic variations while retaining beneficial ones. But natural selection is much more than a negative process because it also generates novelty by increasing the probability of otherwise extremely improbable genetic combinations. In this way, natural selection is a creative process in the sense that while it does not "create" the entities upon which it operates, it does produce adaptive and functional genetic combinations in living organisms that could not have existed in any other way.

There is no foresight in the operation of natural selection, nor does it operate according to some preconceived plan. It is a strictly impersonal natural process that results from the interaction of the properties of the physical-chemical interactions at work in biological entities. Natural selection does have the appearance of purposefulness, however, because it is contextualized by environmental factors: which organisms reproduce more effectively depends on which genetic variations they possess are useful in the place and time where organisms live. While natural selection does not "anticipate" the environments of living organisms, drastic environmental changes may be too rapid for organisms to adapt too. Species extinction is a common result of natural selection, and more than 99 percent of all species that have ever lived on the Earth have become extinct. Natural selection does not "strive" to produce predetermined kinds of organisms, but only organisms that are adapted to their particular environments.

Christian conceptual dialogue with evolutionary biology has focused on the role of chance and necessity, or in more philosophical language, contingency and determinism, in natural selection. This issue is also hotly debated among biologists. Even so, contemporary evolutionary theory poses serious challenges to both Buddhist and Christian faith and practice. For Christian theological reflection, the challenge is three-fold. First, evolutionary theory asserts that variations leading to the origin and differentiation of species are random, in the sense of being undirected. The apparent absence of intelligent control over the contingencies of evolution suggests that novelty in nature is thoroughly accidental, which means that there is no need for divine governance of biological processes. Today, the source of life's complex variations is attributed to genetic mutation, and most biologists follow Darwin in leaving these variations to "chance." Second, the fact that individual organisms must struggle for survival, as well as that the vast number suffer and lose out in this struggle, points to the absolute indifference of natural selection, which is the mechanism that ruthlessly eliminates weaker organisms. Unimaginable suffering and death is the price for the existence of life itself. Finally, life's experiments have required unimaginable amounts of time for the incredible diversity of species to happen. The fact that evolution requires billions of years to bring into existence intelligent beings capable of understanding this process seems to be clear evidence that neither life nor mind is the result of an intelligent divine plan for the universe.

Most nineteenth-century biologists accepted Darwin's theory, although some, like Louis Agassiz, challenged it by arguing that highly complex individual organs (like the human eye) and ecologically sensitive species (like bees and flowers) cannot evolve through the sort of minute random steps described by Darwin. To survive, Agassiz argued, each modification must be beneficial. But complex organs and organic relationships only work as a whole. They cannot develop in steps. So he proposed that complex organisms reflect intelligent design, and thus, testify to both the existence and reality of God. Agassiz's criticism is a restatement of Paley's argument by design and is still playing itself out in the twenty-first century, particularly among Christian fundamentalists and some Protestant evangelicals, especially in the United States. Since conservative and fundamentalist responses to evolutionary biology are monological rather than dialogical—as are materialist scientific criticisms of religion in defense of evolutionary theory—what follows will focus on liberal Christian theological dialogue with evolutionary biology.[26] This will be followed by a summary of Buddhist responses to evolution, particularly as reflected in Buddhist dialogical engagement with the neurosciences.

Permeating Christian dialogue with physics and evolutionary biology is the question of divine action. This question is certainly evolution's greatest challenge to Christian (and Jewish and Islamic) theology. While there is a great diversity of opinion among liberal Christian writers, they are united by at least four common assumptions. First, all agree that scientific conclusions about natural processes are factual descriptions corresponding to physical reality, but capable of revision. Most are critical realists. Second, all take the Bible seriously, but never literally. This means, for example, that Adam and Eve are not historical human beings, the fall and the flood are not historical events, the universe was not created in six days, and the sun did not stop in its course when Joshua attached the city of Jericho. Because these events are physically impossible, these stories must be interpreted symbolically to determine their theological meanings. Third, all affirm that Christian faith and practice must be reconceived in relation to the realities of religious pluralism, as well as the natural sciences. Fourth, all are open to the practice of interreligious dialogue with the natural sciences as a means of creatively transforming Christian faith and practice.

26. For a fuller analysis of materialist interpretations of evolution and Christian fundamentalist and conservative rejection of evolution, see Ingram, *Buddhist-Christian Dialogue in an Age Science*, 58–62.

Given the number of theologians that have given attention to this issue, it is not possible to give a complete summary of all the important writers in this area. Nor shall I concern myself with creationism and the Intelligent Design movement, since these fundamentalist and/or conservative Christian responses to Darwin are well-known and monological in their rather hostile engagement with the sciences. Instead, I shall focus on two theologians, Arthur Peacocke and John Haught, as a means of illustrating the essential themes of contemporary liberal Christian dialogical reflection on evolutionary biology. Their work in science-religion dialogue has served as a model for other Christian writers in the field.

Arthur Peacocke

Peacocke was a biologist-theologian who worked in the field of biochemistry at the universities of Birmingham and Oxford, and in theology at Cambridge. He argued that the assumption that the relation between science and religion is a "state of warfare" is not only simplistic, but also historically untrue.[27] The fact is the relation between science and religion has always been "symbiotic," even when there have been tensions. This is so because both science and religion are involved in the human quest for intelligibility and meaning, which implied for Peacocke that all faith communities, particularly Christian faith communities, should reflect more profoundly on the experience of nature as described in the natural sciences. Science and religion both seek to understand reality, meaning "the way things really are," which is not to say that either is always successful. Nevertheless, Peacocke argued, there exists some common ground for scientists and theologians to engage in dialogue. Although one can neither prove nor disprove the existence of God or the specific claims of Christian faith and practice about the historical Jesus by means of scientific conclusions about natural processes—the error of natural theology traditions like Paley's—a Christian who takes science seriously may reasonably believe in the existence of God as an "inference to the best explanation." In Peacocke's view, the sciences reinforce the long-held intuition of theists that God is: (1) one; (2) the underlying "ground of being" of all that exists; and (3) the source of the deep unity, interconnectedness, and wholeness of existence.[28]

---

27. Peacocke, *Theology for a Scientific Age*, 19–23.

28. See Peacocke's keynote address published in *Boston Conference Program*, October 21–23, 1998: "Science and the Spiritual Quest: Intersections for Today," 1–7.

For Christians, such intuitions based on biology and physics allow Christians to reasonably affirm that there exists a God who is: (1) one and undergoes unfathomable richness of experience; (2) supremely rational; (3) a sustainer and faithful preserver; (4) a continual creator of an anthropic universe;[29] (5) purposeful; (6) always in process of becoming; (7) able to experience joy and delight in creation; (8) the source of the interplay between indeterminacy and law; (9) "self-limited omnipotent and omniscient"; (10) vulnerable, self-emptying, and self-giving love; and (11) suffering, because God experiences the suffering of all sentient beings, just as God experiences the joys of all sentient beings.[30]

Given these "intuitions," the question that concerned Peacocke was: How, given the role of natural selection operating through chance and necessity over time contextualized by environmental factors, is divine action in the universe possible? Simply identifying God with the universe is problematic because monotheism requires that God is, in some sense, the creator of the universe. Nor is pantheism a viable Christian theological option. But if God's actions come from outside the universe, they will always conflict with natural laws and introduce new energies into closed physical systems, which will set theological reflection in conflict with the natural sciences. Only if God is considered as somehow immanent within the universe can divine action be understood as supplemental to physical events by utilizing their energies and physical structures.

The issue is one of causation. How can God "cause" any event, either as the creator of the universe or as an actor somehow involved in events in the universe? In his reflections on this issue, Peacocke drew upon chaos theory, systems theory, and thermodynamics, which over the past fifty years have revealed the role of top-down causation at work in many physical systems. For example, according to the second law of thermodynamics, in isolated systems undergoing irreversible processes far from equilibrium, the entropy or disorder within such a system always increases. This is the physical reason that no system, including the universe of life forms and the universe itself, is permanent. But simultaneously there also emerge new, more ordered or

29. The anthropic principle is a cosmological theory that asserts the four physical forces of the universe—the electromagnetic force, the strong force, the weak force, and gravity—are so balanced that the universe seems finely tuned for human life, which implies that the universes must be inhabited by beings like us. Or restated differently, life like ours somehow constrains the fundamental physical features of the universe. See Wilson, "The Anthropic Principle."

30. Peacocke, *Theology for a Scientific Age*, 102.

"organized" systems, systems from systems undergoing entropy. This means that in far-from-equilibrium, nonlinear, open systems matter displays a potential to be self-organizing and capable of bringing new forms into existence by the operation of internal forces and properties, now operating under the constraints afforded by their being incorporated into a system, whose properties as a whole now have to be taken into account. In other words, changes at the lower microscopic levels of a physical system occur because of top-down causal influences. For example, the molecules of a cell are what they are because of their incorporation into the system as a whole, that is, the cell, the organ of which the cell is a part, and ultimately the entire body of a living organism. In other words, the whole (the cell) constrains, or sets the boundary conditions of, the bottom-up causal actions of its constituent parts (the cell's quarks, atoms, and molecules). So the whole cannot be reduced to, or entirely explained by, its lower-level constituent parts.

This does not mean that bottom-up causation—explaining the whole in terms of the relations of its constituent parts—is of no scientific value. Peacocke's point is that both forms of causation are scientifically interdependent and that emphasizing either one while ignoring the other leads to the distortions of scientific materialism.[31] Of course theological language is always symbolic, especially in reference to God; but Peacocke appropriated the scientific facts of bottom-up and top-down causal interdependence to reflect on how God's creation of the universe from the Big Bang singularity and God's subsequent interaction with the universe is possible. Just as the human body is the boundary condition for the functioning of its individual cells constrained by environmental factors, one may think of the universe with all its constituent parts as the "body" of God, which was Peacocke's way of thinking about God's immanence in the universe.[32] So the universe is the kind of universe it is because of the way it is constrained by the exquisite balance between the four physical forces holding it together, beginning at Plank time, in such a way that life on Earth began to evolve four billion years ago. The universe is constrained to be the kind of universe it is because God, as the boundary condition of the universe, is immanent "in, with, and under" all things and events at every moment of space-time—just as the evolution of Earth's life forms are

31. Ibid., 52–55.

32. Peacocke does not go as far as Sallie McFague because he thinks this notion runs the risk of ignoring Christian experience of God's nature as transcendent to the universe that God creates, much like an artist transcends a work of art, yet incarnates his or her intention and design into a work of art. See McFague, *Models of God*, 69–77.

constrained by the boundary conditions set by the particular physics of this universe in their individual environmental contexts.

Peacocke's views are not pantheist but panentheist. In his view, God is "in, with, and under" all things and events at every moment of space-time. His views are also similar to process theology's understanding of God's relation to the universe. As a Christian, he thought that God's eternal selfhood (Whitehead's primordial nature of God) always transcends the universe, in much the same way that an artist expresses his or her creative selfhood into a painting or sculpture while remaining ontologically distinct from the work of art. Nevertheless, God's interaction with the universe affects and effects God (Whitehead's consequent nature of God) and conditions how God acts in the universe, just as an artist's creative actions affect and effect the artist. The universe as God's "body" does not mean that God's reality is exhausted by or reduced to the physical properties of the universe.

Of course, all Christian theologians believe that God created the universe and is continually active in guiding the course of the universe's history. This history includes the process of evolution. To explain divine action, Peacocke drew on the experimental evidence of biology by appropriating the notion of "emergence." In the natural sciences, emergence is the view that new and predictable phenomena are not reducible to the subsystems on which they depend, and that newly evolved realities in turn exercise causal influence on the parts out of which they arise. In this sense, according to Peacocke, God engages in top-down, or "whole-part," interaction with the universe, so that divine action is indirect, occurring through a chain of levels acting in a "downward" way.[33]

John Haught

Haught follows a different tact than Peacocke. He argues that the primary challenge of evolution to Christian faith lies in interpretations of scientific conclusions filtered through the screen of the reductionisms of philosophical materialism. In fact, Haught thinks that evolutionary biology is a challenge to all religious traditions because all hold that there exists some point or purpose to the universe, that the cosmos is enshrouded in meaning and purpose to which human beings ought to surrender[34] Given the cruel, hit-and-miss way in which evolution appears to work, is it really feasible for any religious

33. Peacocke, *Theology for a Scientific Age*, chap. 11.
34. Haught, *God after Darwin*, 9.

tradition to think of the universe as grounded in an ordering principle to which their ideas of a sacred reality point? Specifically for Christians, is it feasible that a process that impersonally "creates" the incredible complexities of Earth's life forms through the random interplay of chance and necessity over time through natural selection, all without meaning or the need for a personally sustaining designer, leaves any room for Christian faith in God?

Yet even as evolution constitutes a challenge for contemporary Christian faith and practice, this very challenge also presents an opportunity for creative transformation. The reformulation of Christian theology by means of evolutionary biology is what Haught calls "evolutionary theology," which involves six traditional themes reformulated in light of evolutionary science: (1) creation, (2) eschatology, (3) revelation, (4) grace, (5) divine power, and (6) redemption.[35]

The doctrine of creation is central to Christian faith and practice. Traditionally, "creation" is understood as "original creation" (*creatio originalis*), "ongoing" or "continuing creation" (*creatio continua*), and "new creation" or the "fulfillment of creation" (*creatio nova*). Prior to the cosmological discoveries of physics, cosmology, and biological evolution, continuing creation and the fulfillment of creation were not given much attention by theologians. "Creation" meant that God did something "in the beginning," which, when pushed to extremes, leads to deism, or the view that God created the universe, then left it alone to run its own course according to the natural laws God instituted "in the beginning." But the facts of evolution now allow theology to apprehend an ongoing and constantly new reality because, in a continually changing universe where life is constantly evolving, every day is the dawn of a new creation. So evolution allows theology to acknowledge that the notion of an originally instantaneous and created universe is scientifically and theologically incoherent. Moreover, the universe is an imperfect universe, where great suffering is demanded as the price for life itself. Evil and suffering is the dark side of the universe's continuing creation. No form of creation can occur without suffering. Because of this fact, Christian faith looks toward the future eschatological completion of creation (*creatio nova*).

Eschatology is a type of theological reflection focused on what humanity might hope for as ultimate fulfillment.[36] Haught argues that in an evolutionary context, humanity's hope for final fulfillment must be situated in the wider context of the ongoing creation of the entire universe. That is,

35. For a fuller account of these six themes, see ibid., 37–43.

36. See Teilhard de Chardin, *The Phenomenon of Man*, 257–72.

"after Darwin," the universe can be apprehended as moving toward a future fulfillment that includes the entire sweep of evolution. This was also the view of Pierre Teilhard de Chardin, although Haught does not employ Teilhard's "Omega Point" as a description of the universe's final fulfillment. His point is that evolution fits quite well into the framework of biblical eschatology.

Haught also argues that evolution helps theology to reformulate the idea of revelation. Revelation is not the communication of special propositional information from a divine source of knowledge, but rather the communication of God's own selfhood to persons. So understood, revelation is the process whereby "the infinite" pours God's self fully and without reservation into creation wherever creation occurs. This revelatory outpouring is an expression of God's character as love. But the fulfillment of God's character as love cannot be apprehended instantaneously by a finite cosmos. Such reception can only take place in increments because a finite universe can only adapt itself to an infinite source of love by gradual expansion and ongoing self-transcendence, external manifestations of which might appear to scientists as cosmic and biological evolution.

A theology of grace also makes intelligible the randomness, struggle, and natural selection that form the core of evolutionary theory. The doctrine of grace affirms that God loves the universe and all of its various elements and life forms fully and unconditionally, with no strings attached. By definition, love does not absorb, annihilate, or force itself upon the beloved. Rather, love longs for the beloved to become more than the lover. Love longs for the beloved to become independent. Consequently, a central religious intuition of Christian faith is that God loves the universe so that God's grace entails letting go of the universe itself. Only a relatively independent universe allowed to be itself could be intimate with God. Theologically interpreted, then, evolution is a story of struggle toward and expansive freedom for all living things in the presence of God's self-giving grace. Seen from this point of view, randomness and the undirected features of evolution are essential features of any universe created by a gracious God.

Of all the forms of contemporary theological reflection on the notion of divine power, process theology is the most attentive to evolutionary biology in the way in which it conceives how deeply God is involved with a universe wherein life on Earth meanders, experiments, strives, fails, and sometimes succeeds. In agreement with process theology, Haught understands divine power as "the capacity to influence" so that "persuasive love," rather than coercion, is the defining character of God's power. God is not a deity who magically forces things and events to fulfill divine intentions immediately in miraculous ways that contradict the laws of nature that God created. A coercive deity is one that immature minds often wish for and that scientific skeptics most often have in mind when they assert that evolutionary biology has destroyed theism. But given the nature of God's character as love, God wills the independence of the universe, rather than being a despot who controls every event and wills every outcome.

Haught also agrees with the process theology's claim that a universe given the freedom to become more and more autonomous, even creating itself in the process and eventually attaining human consciousness and freedom, has much more integrity and value than any conceivable universe determined in every aspect by a divine designer. Furthermore, divine power as coercive will is incompatible not only with human freedom but also with the prehuman spontaneity that allowed life to evolve into something other than its creator. So, evolution occurs, according to Haught, because a God of love is also the source of not only order, but also novelty. It is the introduction of novelty into the universe that makes evolution possible. Because God is more interested in novelty than in preserving the status quo, God's will is best understood as the maximization of cosmic beauty and intensity of experience for all living entities. That is, "the epic of evolution is the world's response to God's own longing that it strive toward ever richer ways of realizing aesthetic intensity." [37] By offering a multiplicity of new and rich possibilities to the universe, God sustains and creates the universe continually. Or expressed in Whiteheadian language, God is more interested in "adventure" than preserving the status quo.[38]

Finally, again drawing upon process philosophy, Haught believes that evolutionary biology can support a revised Christian understanding of redemption. The question is, given the perpetual perishing that is structurally part of all cosmic processes, for what can one reasonably hope? For Haught, the answer is the same as that given in biblical traditions and other monotheistic traditions; namely, that God is infinitely responsive to the universe wherever life occurs in the universe. Because God's nature is love, the polar side of which is justice, like any lover, God "feels," or "prehends," the universe and wherever life occurs in the universe by taking it into God's self. God

37. *God After Darwin*, 69.

38. See Whitehead, *Adventures of Ideas*, 252–96, for Whitehead's notion that God's relation to the universe is best conceived as an "adventure" that "lures" all creation to new levels of intensity of experience.

responds to the universe accordingly, so that everything that occurs in the process of evolution is "saved" by being taken eternally into God's own feelings for the universe. As a consequence, even though all things and events are the achievements of evolution, all things and events abide permanently within the everlasting compassion of God.[39]

Of course Peacocke's and Haught's theologies of evolution are not the only examples of Christian conceptual dialogue with evolutionary biology. Nor have I given a complete summary of their positions. Nevertheless, the preceding summaries of their dialogue with evolutionary biology will suffice to make the following point clear: on the surface, at least, evolutionary biology has posed rather difficult conceptual challenges to Christian theological reflection. Christian theologians have had to work hard to meet these challenges, mostly because of the theistic character of Christian faith and practice. However, since Buddhism is a non-theistic tradition, many Buddhists have concluded that evolution poses few, if any, conceptual challenges to Buddhist practice. Indeed, as we shall see, this claim often implies a tacit argument for the superiority of Buddhism to Christianity. Accordingly, what follows in the next section is a brief examination of several Buddhist writers in conceptual dialogue with evolutionary biology. This will be followed by some questions regarding the assumption that the natural sciences, including evolutionary biology pose few, if any, conceptual challenges to Buddhist tradition.

EVOLUTIONARY BIOLOGY: BUDDHIST RESPONSES

According to the standard Buddhist doctrine assumed by all schools of Buddhist faith and practice, the universe is "co-originated" because of the arising and passing away of various causes and conditions. Neither the universe nor humanity is the creation of a designer God. Even so, Buddhist doctrines do not necessarily deny the existence of God or a plurality of gods. The point for Buddhists is that even if God or a plurality of deities truly exists, such beings cannot help persons achieve Awakening. Suffering caused by clinging to the fiction of permanent selfhood is a human problem and requires a human solution. God or gods are of no help. In fact, Buddhists regard the worship of God or gods as merely another form of clinging to an imaginary permanence that generates suffering. Consequently, most Buddhists conclude that there can in principle be no conceptual conflict between Buddhism and science, particularly evolutionary biology. The argument is: Buddhism, like the

39. Haught, *God after Darwin*, 42.

natural sciences, rules out God as a meaningful explanatory category so that Buddhism easily harmonizes with all the natural sciences more than theistic religious traditions.

In point of fact, there is much truth to the widespread opinion that Buddhism and the sciences are compatible. William S. Waldron's view seems typical. He argues that nothing similar to the history of conflict that haunts the history of Christian interaction with the natural sciences can be found in the history of Buddhism. In fact, the general Buddhist opinion is that physics, evolutionary biology, and Buddhism share a common ground on the very issues that some Christians have perceived as a threat to Christian faith and practice. Particularly when the sciences are stripped of materialist metaphysics, the defining assumptions of Buddhism are easily harmonized with contemporary scientific thought.[40] Consequently, most contemporary Buddhist reflection on the natural sciences assumes José Cabézon's "complementary model."[41] Furthermore, Buddhist arguments for these conclusions typically focus on those specializations within evolutionary biology collectively known as the cognitive sciences, all of which appear to Buddhists as particularly consonant with Buddhist practices of meditation. A more extended treatment of Buddhism's and Christianity's dialogues with the cognitive sciences will be offered in chapter 5 in relation to Buddhist-Christian interior dialogue.

SUMMARY OBSERVATIONS

To this date, the conversation between Christian theology and the sciences and Buddhism and the sciences has mostly been a one-way conversation about how Christian tradition or Buddhist tradition might be creatively transformed through conceptual dialogue with the various disciplines of the natural sciences. However, very few scientists are interested in how the sciences can be creatively transformed through conceptual dialogue with any religious tradition, much less Christianity and Buddhism. So at the present time, Buddhist and Christian practice of conceptual dialogue with the natural sciences seems more monological than dialogical. Christian dialogue with the natural sciences has included working scientists in the conversation, but this has not happened much in Buddhist conversation with the sciences. Nor has

40. Waldron, "Common Ground, Common Cause: Buddhism and Science on the Affliction of Society," 146.

41. Cabézon, "Buddhism and Science," 35–68.

Buddhist-Christian dialogue included the natural sciences as a third partner. It is in this context that I make the following summary observations, followed by a proposal regarding how the sciences might benefit from a trilogue with Buddhist and Christian tradition.

First, Christian dialogue with the natural is sciences primarily an agenda item of great importance for theological liberalism. Other strands of the Christian theological spectrum, including fundamentalism, most Protestant evangelical theology, Protestant neo-orthodoxy, and conservative Roman Catholic thought rests on the assumption that theology and the sciences are separate domains. Thus science deals with the physical facts of experience while humanistic disciplines like theology focus on wider areas of experience beyond the facts of physical relationships. Protestant fundamentalist theology assumes a conflict model of the religion-science relationship so that where science and religious doctrines conflict, one must always reject scientific conclusions. The mirror opposite of Christian fundamentalism is "scientism," which assumes a materialist metaphysics that reduces reality to the motions of material events, as illustrated by Richard Dawkins.[42] According to "scientism" or scientific materialism, the wider bodies of human experiences—aesthetic experience, moral experience, religious experience—are essentially epiphenomenal. What is real is matter in motion through external relationships. Science-religion dialogue is impossible for fundamentalist Christian theology or scientific materialism.

Protestant evangelical theology, which is heavily grounded in neo-orthodox traditions going back to Karl Barth, and Catholic conservative theology also tend to regard science and religion as separate domains. Science focuses on physical relationships, while religion focuses on aesthetics, ethics, and the experience of transcendent realities. Therefore, there can be no conflict between religion and science, since each is essentially separate from other. Since science and religion are understood as dualistically separate enterprises, there can be no conflict between them since scientists and theologians are talking about different realities. Nor can scientists and theologians have meaningful cross-disciplinary conversation, so that dialogue between them is impossible. Only Christian theological liberalism, particularly process theology, has engaged the sciences dialogically and has undertaken the task of reformulating the major themes of Christian tradition accordingly.

Second, Buddhist conversation with the natural sciences has taken place mostly among Western Buddhists, although the Dalai Lama has participated

42. See Dawkins, *The Blind Watchmaker*.

in a number of dialogues with scientists over the years and has even stated that should science disprove the truth of Buddhism's defining doctrines, he would cease being Buddhist, although he thought such proof to be highly unlikely. [43] However, no Buddhist experiences the natural sciences as posing any challenges to the structure of Buddhists faith and practice because those Buddhists interested in dialogue with the sciences assume that a fundamental harmony exists between scientific views of physical reality and Buddhist teachings and practice. Indeed, most Buddhists think that the natural sciences support Buddhist teachings and practices, so that the sorts of theological challenges that the sciences have posed for Christian tradition are believed to be non-existent in Buddhism.

But is this really the case? Here, I need to be crystal clear about what I am *not* arguing: (1) that Buddhism is deficient because the natural sciences have not challenged Buddhist doctrines in the same way that the natural sciences have challenged Christian doctrines; (2) that Christian tradition is truer or superior to Buddhist tradition because the current scientific origin narrative can be read as a confirmation of certain Christian doctrines; or (3) that Buddhist dialogue with natural sciences should be modeled after Christian encounter with the natural sciences. Consequently, what follows should be understood as descriptive and a bit tentative. Nevertheless, I have questions as a non-Buddhist.

The challenges of science to Christian tradition have mostly involved the displacement of God's role in nature. Of course the issue for Buddhism is not the displacement of God. Nevertheless, the notion that all living things have evolved through accidental forces of random mutation and natural selection in the struggle for existence seems to raise as many questions regarding fundamental Buddhist doctrines as it does for Christian theology. Is the teaching that since all sentient beings are interdependent, we should experience the suffering of others as our suffering and act to relieve suffering by non-violent expedient means based on an illusion? In a universe where the second law of thermodynamics seems to demand suffering and death as the price for life itself, does it make any sense to say we cause our own suffering by clinging to impermanence and that we can free ourselves of suffering by training ourselves not to cling to permanence? Does universal suffering have anything to do with "clinging?" If the universe really is pointless and without value, can Awakening mean anything more than becoming experientially

43. Tenzin [His Holiness the XIV Dalai Lama], "Understanding and Transforming the Mind."

aware of universal pointlessness? If the universe is valueless, what's the value of Awakening? Are compassion and non-violence merely epiphenomenal fantasies? In a pointless and valueless universe, in what and for what can one reasonably hope?

There is also problem with those who, like Wallace and Mansfield, employ Madhyamika dialects in their dialogue with the natural sciences. The problem begins by claiming that an opponent (whether some science of philosophy) asserts proposition X, which the opponent is said to independently exist of a perceiving mind. The imagined opponent, say a physicist, is unlikely to agree with this characterization. Nevertheless Buddhists typically go on to show the logical incoherence of X and thus reaffirm Emptying. Sometimes this is a criticism of an opponent's views, but often it so distorts those views that it becomes a defense against deeply considering the other's position.

Besides not reflecting how scientists actually understand their work, a fruitful dialogue assumes that each party has something to learn from the other and that the exchange can give deeper insight into individual commitments. Not that a scientist should necessarily become a Buddhist (or a Christian), nor that the Buddhist should embrace science. But when there is one stock answer to all questions (that nothing really exists because everything's empty) then the exchange is predictable and infertile. Rather than refining, sharpening, and deepening Buddhism, we have philosophical isolation and inward turning that focuses on momentary bits of meditative experience. As beautiful and transformative as such inward turning can be, it is not conducive to dialogue with the natural science.

A further problem stems from the way Buddhists like Wallace speak and write about an non-verbal "immutable understanding of the true nature of things as empty" that results from successful practice of meditation. Often, as part of this Awakening experience, it is asserted that one becomes experientially aware of the "ultimate nature of mind." Given such non-verbal immutable understanding and experience, how can dialogue even be possible, either with Christians or with Scientists?

Only Buddhists can answer these questions. They are there to be answered whether or not Buddhists chose to confront them. Doing so in the context of a conceptual trilogue with Christian theology and the natural sciences would, I believe, engender new forms of creative transformation in both Buddhist and Christian tradition, and possibly even the natural sciences. At this point, exactly how remains an open question, since the sciences have not as yet been included as dialogical partners in current Buddhist-Christian conceptual encounter. Part of the problem is that most Buddhist and Christian dialogue with the natural sciences has been a one-sided affair that focuses mostly on how Buddhists and Christians might benefit from conversation with the sciences. Little attention has been paid to how the sciences might benefit from dialogue with Buddhism and Christianity, much less from a trilogue with Buddhist and Christian traditions. The structure of authentic dialogue is at least a two-way, give-and-take conversation. But for the most part, Buddhist and Christian dialogue with the sciences exhibits a one-way monological structure. If "creative transformation" names what happens when Buddhists, Christians, and scientists are open to appropriating insights of the other into their own perspectives, how might the sciences be creatively transformed through dialogue with Buddhist and Christian traditions?

Mickael Stenmark argues that there are four ways in which "religious world views" could and should make substantial contributions to the development of the natural sciences: (1) shaping the "problem-stating phase," of scientific inquiry, (2) shaping the "developmental phase" of science, (3) shaping the "justification phase" of science, and (4) shaping the "application phase" of science.[44] For the purpose of illustration, I will focus on the problem-stating phase.

In common with scholars of other disciplines, scientists must first decide what is worth studying. The issue is how scientists want to spend their professional time, energy, and their own and other people's economic resources on their various research projects. Imre Lakatos writes that the sciences should be autonomous in the sense that the direction of research should proceed unhindered and undetermined by ideological or religious interests. Accordingly, the wider society beyond the scientific community should never be allowed to determine the choice of scientific problems and research areas. Lakatos' concern was that the integrity of science is always threatened by political interests and often by religious interests.[45]

This is a conclusion with which Buddhists and Christians should easily concur. People and groups in power—governments, corporations, religious institutions—often decide the kind of research agendas scientists should pursue and which agendas should be ignored. A contemporary American example of this is the denial of federal funding for stem cell research by the federal government motivated by the desire of George W. Bush's administration to win support from conservative evangelical and fundamentalist Christian

44. Stenmark, *How to Relate Science and Religion*, 216.
45. Lakatos, *Mathematics, Science, and Epistemology*, vol. 2, 258.

organizations. In cases like this, scientists often have to make the difficult choice between doing their research under these conditions or not doing it at all. The fact is that under current political conditions, the sciences have become heavily politicized and often religiously and ideologically partisan.

Furthermore, certain areas that rich but not poor people, whites but not people of color, men but not women, Christians but not non-Christians, liberals but not conservatives are interested in will often determine what scientists decide to investigate or choose not to investigate. For example, Richard Dawkins has stated that his choice of research interests in biology derives from his wish to be an "intellectually fulfilled atheist," which he thinks Darwin made possible, and from his intention to employ his scientific research to defend atheism against all forms of religion, particularly theism.[46]

However, it is one thing for working scientists who are committed to say, Buddhism, Christianity, Islam, or atheistic naturalism to be influenced by their worldview commitments in the selection of research agendas. But it is quite another thing when religious people, politicians, or non-scientifically trained people are allowed to ideologically determine the agenda of scientific research. The question is, should worldview influence on science be illuminated from the practice of science? The answer is that this is not possible. Scientific development may even at times benefit from such influence because some topics, some research programs, some things that require explanation might not be noticed by working scientists because of the particular worldview influencing their work. Therefore it seems quite reasonable to affirm religious and/or philosophical motives to guide the kinds of research scientists pursue, particularly when scientists themselves set their research agendas. The real question is, what kinds of religious assumptions, worldviews, or ideologies should influencing scientific research?

Here, Buddhist-Christian conceptual dialogue with the natural sciences might aid in clarifying uncritically assumed theological, philosophical, or ideological assumptions at work in scientific agendas, which in turn might engender more critical self-awareness of ideological interpretations of science that cannot be coherently supported by scientific methods or the objects of scientific research. More specifically, the reductionisms of scientific materialism might not be so easily assumed by many working scientists if they were more critically aware of reductionist presuppositions that explain by explaining away whole areas of experience—music, beauty, love, ethical sensitivity, longings for justice, self-consciousness, and religious experience—as

46. Dawkins, *The Blind Watchmaker*, 6.

the motions of physical events. Buddhist-Christian conceptual dialogue with the natural sciences would serve scientists well as a reminder that scientific methods and conclusions are relevant to only small domains of physical reality. As important as these domains are, they do not constitute the totality of the structure of existence.

At the same time, however, neither Buddhist nor Christian doctrines or practices have any authority in themselves for setting research agendas or in deciding scientific questions. Furthermore, not all forms of Buddhism or Christianity are able to dialogically engage the sciences because they are ideologically anti-science. Examples abound: forms of popular Buddhism that stress karmic causes of physical and mental illness and the need for changing the cause-effect relations governing one's personal life in order to be cured of these illnesses are not conducive to dialogue with the sciences; Christian forms of fundamentalism; the Intelligent Design movement; or apocalyptic forms of Christian theology are not conducive to dialogue with the natural sciences, let alone dialogue with non-Christian religious traditions.

But mainline forms of Buddhism and Christianity are quite capable of making meaningful contributions to the practice of science through dialogue. For example, Buddhist tradition affirms that all things and events at every moment of space-time are interdependently related, so that no thing or event is separate from any other thing or event. One conclusion Buddhists draw from this doctrine is that because we are so interdependently linked, the suffering of any sentient being is the suffering of all sentient beings. Consequently, Buddhists can reasonably ask scientists to refrain from conducting any kind of research that could be harmful to human and non-human life. Similarly, Buddhist interest in ecology, also motivated by universal compassion, might inspire more scientific research into the biological structures that support Buddhist views on the environment.[47]

The Christian doctrine of the incarnation of the Logos in the historical Jesus as the Christ, particularly as read through the filter of the prologue of the Gospel of John, can also be read as a ringing declaration of the interdependence of all things and events originating in the creative action of God, both in the origins of the universe and in God's continuing creative activity in the present. Christians inspired by this interpretation of the incarnation and the doctrine of creation might also be inspired to ask scientists to refrain from research that is harmful to life. This in turn can promote scientific research as a means to attaining economic, social, and gender justice for all human beings,

47. On this point, see Sponberg, "Green Buddhism and the Hierarchy of Compassion."

ecological justice for both human and other sentient beings, along with the creation of technology that decreases the violence persons impose on one another and on the environment. Another important example is Christian encouragement of stem cell research, of which's there are numerous examples not often noted in American news media.[48]

What the natural sciences tell us is that all interpretations of experience are limited and partial, which means that neither science, nor Buddhism, nor Christianity can offer a complete account of reality, "the way things really are." The universe seems quite pluralistic in structure, from the smallest dimension of quantum events, to the very large structures of the universe, to the universe itself. Different theoretical frameworks may better represent different aspects of reality. If one believes in God, God's relation to impersonal objects like stars and planets differs from God's relation to persons and sentient beings. If one is a Buddhist, the non-personal dimensions of existence can seem to support Buddhist notions of Awakening. The point is that the pursuit of coherence must not ignore the differences between scientific, Buddhist, and Christian accounts of reality. Engaging in a science, Buddhist, and Christian trilogue will involve the use of a diversity of theoretical constructions in order to prevent the sort of fundamentalism that occurs when we take any one theoretical framework too literally. Perhaps a more inclusive theoretical framework, yet to be discovered, may come to light because of this trilogue that might even unify scientific, Buddhist, and Christian knowledge and practice.

48. For a convincing theological argument supporting stem cell research see Peters, *Science, Theology, and Ethics*, chap. 9.

4

Buddhist-Christian
Socially Engaged Dialogue

Although Buddhists have emphasized socially engaged dialogue with Christians more than conceptual dialogue, Christian conceptual dialogue with Buddhists has also generated interest in the relevance of Buddhist thought and practice to issues of social, environmental, economic, and gender justice. Such Christian interest is generated by a two-thousand-year history of Christian social activism. Since issues of social, economic, gender and ecological violence and injustice are systemic, global, interconnected, and interdependent, they are neither religion-specific nor cultural-specific. All human beings have experienced these forms of oppression. Accordingly, Christians and Buddhists have mutually apprehended common experiences and resources for working together to liberate human beings and nature from the global forces of systemic oppression. *engaged Buddhism*

Thich Nhat Hanh is given credit for coining the term "social engagement" in 1963 as a description of the Buddhist anti-war movement in Vietnam. But in fact, the Buddhist Renewal Movement in Vietnam first coined this term as *nham gian Phat Giao* in the 1930s.[1] Nevertheless, because of Thich Nhat Hanh's leadership of the Buddhist anti-war movement in the 60s, "social engagement" is now the most common term describing Buddhist social activism.[2] Some Christian liberation theologians have also appropriated

1. Rawlings-Way, "Religious Interbeing: Buddhist Pluralism and Thich Nhat Hanh," 56.

2. According to Kraft, *Inner Peace, World Peace*, 18, Thich Nhat Hanh published a book by this title in 1963. While I have not seen this text or any other scholarly reference to it, Christopher S. Queen notes that the French term *engagé*, meaning "politically

this term as a designation of Christian social activism. The heart of Buddhist social engagement is interdependence and non-violence. Interdependence (*pratīya-samuptpāda* or "dependent co-arising") is the doctrine that all things and events at every moment of space-time are constituted by their interrelationships with all other things and events, so that nothing exists in separation from other things and events. All things and events are mutually co-created by this web of interrelationships. Since these relationships are always in a state of change and process, all things and events are in a constant state of change and becoming. Impermanence is therefore ingredient in the structure of existence itself.

Part of the meaning of Awakening (*nirvāna*) is experiential awareness of dependent co-arising, which in turn engenders "compassion" (*karuṇā*) for all sentient beings. Compassion originates from awareness, engendered by the practice of meditation, that in a mutually interdependent universe, the suffering of others is the suffering of all, which in turn energizes action to relieve sentient beings from suffering. Compassionate non-violence is the ethical heart of Buddhist social activism.

Socially engaged Buddhists are uncompromising in the practice of nonviolence, and for Christians this has raised questions about justice. Justice is a central theological category in Christian social activist traditions, but the notion of justice has not played an equivalent role in Buddhism. Christian tradition gives priority to loving engagement with the world as the foundation for establishing justice. So for Christians, the question is to what extent is nonviolent compassion toward all sentient beings, even to aggressors doing harm to whole communities of persons, itself an occasion for injustice?[3] While justice is not identical with revenge, Christian traditions of social justice demand that those who do harm not get away with it, which means that the establishment of justice may necessitate the use of violent means.[4]

---

outspoken" or "politically involved," was common among activist intellectuals in French Indochina long before the 1960s. Queen, "Introduction."

3. Cf. Cobb, *Beyond Dialogue*, chaps. 4–5; as well as Keenan, "Some Questions about the World"; and Keenan, "The Mind of Wisdom and Justice in the Letter of James"—two important examples of contemporary Christian dialogue with Buddhists on the relation between non-violent compassion and love as the center of Christian traditions of social justice.

4. An important exception to this is the Quaker tradition of social activism, which does not include the use of violence for any reason as a means of resolving social justice issues. More than most mainline Christian denominations, Quaker practice and social activism are modeled after the historical Jesus' injunction to "turn the other cheek" when confronted with an aggressor.

Consequently, while the practice of non-violent compassion as the ethical norm for Buddhist social engagement has forced Christians to reexamine the relationship between love, justice, and violence, love as involvement with the world in the struggle for justice has energized Buddhists to examine the relation between the practice of non-violent compassion and justice. Indeed, a current question that Buddhists have been debating because of dialogue with Christians is whether a distinctively Buddhist concept of justice is even possible. Christian notions of justice currently assume Western Enlightenment notions of separate individuals having permanent rights, but little responsibility for community well-being, which Buddhists think contradicts the principle of interdependence. Yet both Christians and Buddhists seem agreed that working together to resolve justice issues is not only possible, but also necessary even as the foundations of Buddhist social engagement and Christian social activist traditions are not identical.

Although a number of theologians are in dialogue with Buddhist traditions of social activism, Paul F. Knitter is perhaps the best-known Christian thinker currently socially engaged in dialogue with Buddhists. Drawing on Christian liberation theology, Knitter believes there exists a common context from which religious persons of different traditions, in this case Christianity and Buddhism, can and should enter into dialogue. Knitter identifies this common context with Christian liberation theology's assertion of "the *preferential option for the poor and non-person*, meaning the option to work with and for the victims of this world."[5] Furthermore, Knitter argues, apart from commitment to and identification with the poor and the oppressed in the global struggle for justice, conceptual dialogue between Christians and Buddhists remains an academic elitist enterprise with little relevance to the lives oppressed persons.

In point of fact, Christians and Buddhists have recognized poverty and oppression as common problems from which human beings need liberation. It is necessary, therefore, that Buddhist-Christian dialogue evolve into a shared commitment to the liberation of human beings from all forms of oppression. In the struggle for liberation, Christians and Buddhists share a common ground that enables them to hear one another and be mutually transformed in the process. Thus while it is important for Christians and Buddhist to engage conceptually, Knitter concludes that such dialogue is irrelevant apart from socially engaged dialogue grounded in the preferential option for the

5. Knitter, "Towards a Liberation Theology of Religions," 185.

poor and the non-person.[6] However, socially engaged dialogue, particularly with regard to economic and environment issues, also needs to be grounded in conceptual dialogue with the natural sciences. For example, confronting the economic oppression that breeds poverty and destroys environmental systems necessitates a critique of free market capitalism established on deep knowledge of environmental and ecological forces, which requires conceptual dialogue with economics and evolutionary biology.

Because of the growing popularity of Thich Nhat Hanh's thought, both Buddhists and non-Buddhists, especially in Europe and the United States, picked up the term "engaged Buddhism" as a description of something that had not occurred before in Buddhist history. So the first question to be addressed is why this should be the case. Is there anything new in "engaged Buddhism" that has not been characteristic of previous Buddhist history? I shall argue that while the term "engaged Buddhism" is new, it points to traditions of ethical discipline and social activism that have always been central to Buddhist thought and practice. What is new about "engaged Buddhism" is what this term means in its present contemporary context. To see this, it is necessary to engage in a critique of traditional Western assumptions about ethics that predominate in Western philosophy and currently govern most Christian ethical and social discourse.

THREE WESTERN PHILOSOPHICAL OBSTACLES

As George Dreyfus notes, even when Western interpreters notice that Buddhist meditational practices are relevant to ethical self-discipline and social engagement, they incorrectly tend to view social activism as something quite external to Buddhist experience of awakening.[7] Thus, most Christians interpret *sīla* ("morality") mainly as a set of injunctions to avoid certain kinds of conduct, such as the five precepts emphasized in Theravada tradition or the ten virtues emphasized in Tibetan tradition, that help Buddhists gradually withdraw from the world into a private experience of an enlightenment that detaches individuals from social and worldly care. Three assumptions seem to guide this view.

First, most contemporary Western ethical theories assert that ethics is primarily about rules and injunctions, while less concerned with the development of good character. This assumption is particularly common to utilitarian

6. Ibid., 185–86.

7. Dreyfus, "Meditation as Ethical Activity."

theories, which emphasize choosing the right course of action for the sake of the greatest happiness for the greatest number. Notions of injunctions and rightness are also emphasized in deontological theories. Deontology, associated with Kant, holds that the goodness of moral life does not consist in the development of human qualities such as good character, but consists in the ability to act according universal moral laws. Thus, to be moral is to decide to act upon certain agreed rules of action—the maxims that conform to these universal moral laws.

Second, most Western ethical theory asserts the duality of reason and emotion, along with the privileging of reason. This dualism is strongly characteristic of Kantian traditions of ethical theory. To perhaps oversimplify, we cannot help what we feel, but only what we do. So no one can be said to have a duty to feel certain emotions or to act from certain emotions. Ethics must be understood as a system of obligations. Since emotions cannot be made objects of obligations, they are without ethical relevance. Neither their presence nor their absence can reflect on a person's morality, since they are outside the scope of personal responsibility. Seen from this point of view, ethics becomes the exploration of the rationality of limited decisions reached through weighting the advantages or disadvantages of alternatives, all in isolation from human emotional experiences and human participation in religious or cultural traditions.

Third, most contemporary ethical theory asserts a duality between external agency and internal attitudes. Here again, the Kantian tradition is representative of the widely shared Western view that ethics concerns the domain of external action, not the realm of internal emotions. So ethics and social activism become a matter of thinking clearly, and then proceeding to outward dealings with other human beings. But the attitudes we have or the emotions we experience in these dealings are ethically irrelevant. To be moral does not mean to possess good human qualities, as in most traditional cultures and in Buddhist tradition, but to choose the right course of action.

In contrast to most Western ethical theory, the aim of Buddhist ethics is to *become* virtuous, not merely to adhere to objective moral rules arrived at rationally. Hence Buddhism stresses the practice of meditation in personal moral cultivation as foundational for the practice of social engagement. Accordingly, Western virtue-ethics approaches—those that originate in Platonic and Aristotelian philosophy, but are now out of fashion—rather than the utilitarian or deontological approaches of most contemporary Western ethical teaching, might provide Christians a more useful hermeneutical bridge from which to dialogically encounter Buddhist traditions of social engagement. Accordingly, as a thought experiment, I shall assume a virtue ethics approach as a heuristic devise through which to examine and interpret the ethical sources of traditional Buddhist activism, now referred to as "Buddhist social engagement."

THE STRUCTURE OF BUDDHIST SOCIAL ENGAGEMENT

No current writer has written about the structure of Buddhist social engagement more clearly than Sallie B. King. She describes Buddhist and Christian social activism as "spiritual social activism," which excludes those who use their participation in a religious tradition to justify hatred, aggression, or violence—which she thinks are expressions of secularism even when engaged in by Buddhists or Christians.[8] She notes that socially engaged dialogue between Buddhists and Christians has been ongoing since the end of the nineteenth century. Of course, although he was not a Buddhist, Mahatma Gandhi was the pioneer of what King calls "spiritual social activism," which has deeply inspired both Buddhist and Christian social activism.

Any survey of the mutual influence of Gandhi's philosophy of non-violence on Buddhist-Christian socially engaged dialogue would note that a Christian organization, the Fellowship of Reconciliation, was heavily involved in supporting the Buddhist-anti-war movement in Vietnam. Christian influence has entered into Asian Buddhist countries through such Buddhist leaders as Dr. Bhimrao Ambedkar, Thich Nhat Hanh, Sulak Sivraaksa, and Aung San Suu Kyi, all of whom spent considerable time in Europe and North America and received some of their education in these regions. Other Buddhist leaders, such as the Dalai Lama and Daisaku Ikeda, who did not spend their formative years outside their countries, are in constant dialogue with Western religious and secular leaders. It was Thich Nhat Hanh who convinced Martin Luther King Jr. to include protest against the Vietnam War in the agenda of the American Civil Rights movement. Martin Luther King returned the favor by nominating Thich Nhat Hanh for the Nobel Peace Prize. The Quaker organization the American Friends Service Committee later nominated Sulak Sivaraksa for the same prize. Daniel Berrigan and Thomas Merton were deeply influenced by Thich Nhat Hanh.

But Buddhist social engagement in all its forms has its particular defining structure, just as Christian social activism has its particular structure. What

8. King, "Buddhism and Social Engagement," 159–62.

follows is a description of the specific character of Buddhist social engagement and Christian social activism. In doing so, I will focus on three interdependent elements that characterize Buddhist social engagement as "Buddhist."[9]

First, Buddhist social engagement in all its forms affirms that one must, according to Thich Nhat Hanh, "be peace" in order to "make peace."[10] Or as the Dalai Lama has said, "Everyone loves to talk about calm and peace whether in family, national or international contexts, but without *inner* peace, how can we make peace real?"[11] Since, according to Buddhist teachings, everything is interdependent, working for peaceful social change expressive of compassionate non-violence requires the practice of meditation. This is the meaning of Thich Nhat Hanh's formula, "outer work involves inner work." The point is that one who has experienced reality—the way things really are—as interdependent simultaneously sees through the falsehood of separate selfhood. The result is that things and events, including forms of injustice, are apprehended truly without illusion, so that one's social activism accurately reflects the realities of particular situations. In Buddhist experience, literally, one's self is never separate from the other; no human being is ever separate from another human being; the oppressed is never separate from the oppressor. The Buddhist term for this experiential apprehension is "non-self" (*anatta* in Pali; *anātman* in Sanskrit).

Second, this means Buddhist understanding of compassion is not only grounded in the doctrine of interdependence, but also the doctrine of nonself. Cultivating experiential awareness selflessness is foundational to Buddhist spirituality and is a core theme in all traditions of Buddhism. Consequently, selflessness and compassionate action in social engagement are two interdependent sides of a single doctrine. Accordingly, the practice of meditation is the "skillful means" (*upāya*) through which one seeks to eradicate one's preoccupation with oneself so that one can cultivate an experiential recognition of the sameness of one's own and others' value and one's own wishes for the well-being of those others. The social ethical result of such personal self-transformation is that one naturally works for the well-being of another as easily as one works for one's own well-being because, literally, one *is* the other. The well-being of others constitutes our individual well-being even if the

9. My explanations of these elements are based on King's analysis in "Buddhism and Social Engagement," 162–77.

10. See Nhat Hanh, *Being Peace*.

11. Tenzin, *The World of Tibetan Buddhism*, 85.

others are immoral persons or oppressors. Or as Thich Nhat Hanh describes the non-duality between victim and oppressor:

> One day [during the crisis of the Vietnamese boat people] we received a letter telling us about a young girl on a small boat who was raped by a Thai pirate. She was only twelve, and she jumped into the ocean and drowned herself.
>
> When you first learn of something like that, you get angry at the pirate. You naturally side with the girl. As you look more deeply you will see differently. If you take the side of the little girl, then it is easy. You only have to take a gun and shoot the pirate. But we cannot do that. In my meditation I saw that if I had been born in the village of the pirate and raised in the same conditions as he was, I am now the pirate. I cannot condemn myself so easily.

Thich Nhat Hanh's poem about this event, "Call me By My True Name," reads in part:

> I am the 12–year old girl, refugee on a small boat,
> who throws herself into the ocean after being raped by a sea pirate,
> and I am the pirate, my heart not yet capable of seeing and loving.
> My joy is like spring, so warm it makes flowers bloom in all Walks
>   of life.
> My pain is like a river of tears, so full it fills up the four Oceans.
> Please call me by my true names,
> so I can hear all my cries and laughs at once,
> so I can see that my joy and pain are one.
> Please call me by my true names,
> so I can wake up,
> and so the door of my heart can be left open,
> the door of compassion.[12]

Third, the concept of *karma* plays an important role in enforcing Buddhist attitudes about the practice of non-violence. Sallie King notes that the law of karma ("causation") affects Buddhist practice of non-violence in two ways: (1) the role karma plays in the construction of one's present and future identity, and (2) violent reaction against a person that does injury, that is, returning violence with violence, always causes negative results for both the receiver of violence and the perpetrator of violence. The result of all violent actions, even in violent self-defense against an aggressor, merely adds

---

12. Naht Hanh, *Being Peace*, 61–64; also quoted in King, "Buddhist Social Engagement," 165.

to the spiraling cycle of violence. Or as the *Dhammapada* points out, "Hatred is never appeased by hatred in this word; it is appeased by love. This is an eternal law."[13] The Dalai Lama as leader of the Tibetan liberation movement illustrates this point. He strongly rejects violent response to the Chinese invasion Tibet. In his words

> Anger, jealousy, impatience, and hatred are the real troublemakers; with them problems cannot be solved. Though one may have temporary success, ultimately one's hatred or anger will create further difficulties. With anger, all actions are swift. When we face problems with compassion, sincerely and with good motivation, it may take longer, but ultimately the solution if better, for there is far less chance of creating a new problem through the temporary "solution" of the present one.[14]

The doctrinal foundations of Buddhist social engagement, with its emphasis on the practice of meditation as a necessary foundation for social activism, is the primary focus of Christians socially engaged in dialogue with Buddhists. To understand the nature of this dialogue it will be necessary to reflect on the structure of Christian social activism. The question is, what makes Christian social activism *Christian*? What follows is a reflection on this question in conversation with the structure of Buddhist social engagement.

THE STRUCTURE OF CHRISTIAN SOCIAL ACTIVISM

As a Christian historian of religions engaged in dialogue with Buddhists, I am frequently annoyed by uncritical caricatures some Christian scholars too regularly foist upon Buddhist tradition. Such caricatures are probably unintentional and their purposes usually benign. Yet caricatures persist in scholarly Christian discourse about Buddhist tradition. Since these occur in the work of Christians who admire Buddhist tradition and seek to learn from it, they are all the more distorting and uninformed.

One caricature that still haunts Christian encounter with Buddhist faith and practice is the ahistorical assumption that Buddhist tradition as a whole is socially unengaged, and therefore in need of serious reformation through dialogue with Christian tradition. Important Buddhist teachers and philosophers have also bought into this caricature. For example, Masao Abe, in relation to justice issues, wrote: "But some Buddhist thinkers, including

13. *Dhammapada*, translated in Rahula, *What the Buddha Taught*, 126.
14. Tenzin, *Kindness, Clarity, and Insight*, 62.

myself, are aware that Buddhism must develop itself through confrontation with Christianity. It may not be related to the most fundamental point. But with such problems as that of justice and the understanding of history in regard to justice, I think Buddhists must learn from Christianity, because the idea of justice is very weak and unclear in Buddhism."[15]

An influential example of this caricature of Buddhist tradition is also at work in the theology of Abe's main Christian dialogical partner, John Cobb. In comparing the ethical and social implications of Buddhist and Christian universalism, Cobb notes that despite many striking parallels, Buddhist and Christian teachings make different universal claims. According to Buddhist teaching, Gautama is one of many embodiments of Buddha Nature, so that nothing similar to the once-and-for-all uniqueness of the historical Jesus is asserted about the historical Buddha.[16] The claim that the Buddha Nature is in all things and events—a Mahayana, not a Theravada teaching—and that the enlightenment attained by Gautama is the proper goal of all sentient beings is different than Christian claims about the resurrection of the historical Jesus. Consequently, the "structure of Buddhist existence" is not the same as the "structure of Christian existence."[17]

For Cobb, this implies that Buddhist practice and experience have broken the dominance of the self or the "I" because all boundaries and distinctions between self and other are ontologically canceled out at the moment of enlightenment. In so doing, Buddhist experience frees persons from anxiety and egoistic self-concern. Thereby, Buddhists are able to achieve a unique openness to the structures of reality. Christian tradition, however, heightens self-transcendence by objectifying one's self as separate from other selves. Thus Christians are taught that individual selves can and should assume responsibility for what they do and for what they are. Consequently, Cobb thinks there is fuller ethical and social consciousness in Christian experience than in Buddhist experience.[18]

For this reason, in Cobb's opinion, the Christian notion of love (*agapē*) is different from the Buddhist notion of compassion (*karuṇā*). In Mahayana tradition especially, when non-attachment is attained, the bodhisattva is thereby filled with compassionate empathy for the suffering of all unenlightened

15. Abe and Cobb, "Buddhist-Christian Dialogue," 24.

16. Cobb, *Christ in a Pluralistic Age*, 206.

17. See Cobb, *The Structure of Christian Existence*, 16–17, for his definition of "structure of existence."

18. Cobb, *Christ in a Pluralistic Age*, 208–9.

sentient beings. But even though this is a "beautiful idea," Cobb thinks the Christian notion of love is ethically more sensitive to issues of social justice. *Agapē*, he writes, centers on awareness of selves involved with, yet ontologically independent of, other selves. It also implies ontological separation between human selves and the self of God. Since selves in separation from God are in a state of sin, no self can become virtuous through living an ethically good life. However a morally good life might be conceived, sinful selves do not establish it in relation to other selves or to God by any form of moral behavior or social activism. Since salvation is a gift of God's graceful *agapē*, moral and social behavior is Christian only if it expresses gratitude for what God's loving grace has bestowed on the self. That is, Christians have moral and social obligations to be performed as expressions of gratitude; performing moral and social obligations do not make one good, since all selves, even selves graced by God, remain in a state of sin.

Consequently, *agapē* seems to Cobb to be less "defused" than *karuṇā*, and therefore ethically and socially more relevant to the life experiences of selves existing separately, yet interactively, in the world. Accordingly, he believes that *agapē* has historically provided norms of ethical and social organization that are more fully developed in Christian tradition than in Buddhist tradition.[19]

While at first glance there seems to be much in the formative Theravada and Mahayana lineages of Buddhism that supports Cobb's interpretation of Buddhist teaching and practice, in fact what Buddhists now call "social engagement," while conceived differently than Christian ethical-social teaching, has always been at the heart of Buddhist teaching, practice, and experience. That is, ethics and social engagement have played as important a role in Buddhist teaching and practice as ethics and social activism have played in Christian teaching and practice. Indeed, Buddhist Awakening is never an unethical event that withdraws an awakened one from engagement with the needs of society at large. The same is true for the practice of Christian faith: salvation is never an unethical or socially unengaged event.

In fairness, it must be also emphasized that Cobb's point is not that actual Buddhists are less moral or less loving than actual Christians. His point is that as Christian faith can be theologically transformed by appropriating Buddhist denials of substance categories in reference to the self, so Buddhist tradition can be ethically transformed by appropriating Christian notions of

19. Ibid., 215–18. Abe also agrees with Cobb's assessment. See his conversation with Cobb in "Buddhist-Christian Dialogue," 13–29.

transcendence and thereby deepen its tradition of social activism. [20] This is a valid conclusion, yet often as I have participated in dialogical discussions between Buddhists and Christians on such issues as the environment, justice, poverty, or violence, it is easier for me to identify a distinctively Buddhist position than a distinctively Christian position. Certainly, the problem may be my own, but I often have difficulty identifying what makes a particular form of social activism Christian and not something else, say, Jewish, Islamic, of Buddhist. Buddhists seem as compassionate and loving as Christians; Buddhists seem as concerned about justice, economic exploitation, and environmental degradation as Christians; Buddhists seem as concerned about peace as Christians. The Christian notion of agapic love of one's neighbors can be, and often is, affirmed by Buddhists; compassion for all suffering beings is recognized and celebrated by much Christian ethical and social teaching.

Part of the problem has to do with the philosophical assumptions underlying much Christian ethical and social teaching. For example, many Christian theologians view Buddhist notions of social engagement through the filter of Western utilitarian or Kantian deontological theory rather than Western traditions of virtue ethics that originated with Plato and Aristotle. This means that "Christian ethics" often seems to be more a matter of duty than of virtue, since the stress of much contemporary Christian theological discourse and social activism is on performing obligations consistent with the revelation of God's love to humanity embodied in the events surrounding the historical Jesus. At least from a Protestant perspective, Christian ethics and social activism, unlike Buddhist teaching, do not normally demand that persons become virtuous. [21] Nor is meditation or contemplative prayer a required ingredient of ethical behavior or social activism. One does not often hear in Christian teaching that "outer work involves inner work."

I usually do not experience the same difficulty understanding what makes traditions of ethics and social engagement Buddhist. Buddhist traditions of social engagement are bound to a specific worldview in which the doctrines of dependent co-origination and non-self are defining teachings that distinguishes Buddhism from other religious traditions. This means that the

---

20. See my fuller critique of Cobb's dialogue with Buddhism in "To John Cobb," 8.

21. However, contemporary Catholic theory, rooted in the theology of Thomas Aquinas, whose ethical thought in turn was grounded in Aristotle's ethics, has engendered Catholic understanding, and deep appreciation for, Buddhist social engagement. For an excellent discussion of the differences between Protestant and Roman Catholic ethics, see Gustafson, *Protest and Roman Catholic Ethics.*

core of Buddhist ethical and social teachings is a strong sense of the intimate, organic interrelatedness of all sentient beings. Accordingly, Buddhists are led from rigid distinctions that cut off individuals from creative social relationships to an openness that is fully aware of the dynamic interrelatedness of all things and events at every moment of space-time. Furthermore, awareness of interdependency does not blur awareness of differences of personal, social, and historical distinctions and identities. Rather, the experience of universal interdependence enables compassion to flow more freely in creative interaction with others through recognizing that while others are different, they remain tightly bound together in the universal web of interrelationships that constitute the whole of reality.

Other than the fact that Christian tradition's worldview is monotheistic and Buddhism's is not, there is little in Buddhist teachings about social engagement that contradicts Christian ethics and social activism. Perhaps the solution to my dilemma concerning what makes Christian social activism Christian and Buddhist social engagement Buddhist can be resolved by a lesson I have learned from the history of religions: people understand reality through narratives. That is, religious traditions work through narratives and religious people constantly reinterpret these narratives, thereby gaining new insight to engage issues that a religious tradition's narratives could not have foreseen in their earlier histories. Sometimes ignoring, or even rejecting, part of a tradition's narrative that is deemed irrelevant is part of these reinterpretations. Either way, understanding a religious tradition, one's own or someone else's, means grappling with its foundational narratives.[22]

It is their narratives that distinguish Christian social activist traditions from Buddhist traditions of social engagement. It seems cleat that contemporary Buddhist traditions of social engagement have reclaimed aspects of the Dharma that have always existed in order to address issues of injustice in a new way. Similarly, Christian activists in the late nineteenth and early twentieth centuries focused on neglected aspects of the Bible to preach a social gospel of engagement with the world—a focus continuing in Christian liberation theologies minus the Social Gospel's optimism about human nature.

Of course, there are many more stories in Buddhism's narrative tradition than in Christianity's narrative tradition. The number of texts comprising the Buddhist canon is immense, more like a library. Christians have a one-volume narrative anthology—the Bible—and most of the narratives come from the Hebrew texts. John Dominic Crossan has pointed out that Christian tradi-

22. See Keenan, "Some Questions about the World," 181–85.

tion transmuted many of the parables into moral allegories, while the original teller of the parables, the historical Jesus, became the parable of God.[23] This is why the defining Christian narrative is eschatological. Christians experience the universe as moving toward a last age, to a final fulfillment, to what Teilhard de Chardin called the "Omega point." The universe is going somewhere, lured by God to achieve its final consummation. The value of the universe for Christians is grounded on the doctrine of the incarnation: in the life, death, and resurrection of the historical Jesus, God took upon God's self the conditions of finite existence imposed by the history and the realities of physics and biology, and continues doing so through the Holy Spirit until God's intention in creation is fulfilled. Of course, there is a great deal of disagreement and discussion about this aspect of the Christian narrative within the history of Christian theological reflection.

Buddhism's defining narratives present a very different version of the universe. Buddhist teachings place no emphasis on the historical movement of the universe toward a final consummation. Indeed, Buddhist tradition celebrates the absence of teleological assumptions in its teachings. The doctrine of dependent co-origination, for example, teaches that existence commences with ignorance, which leads to old age and death, only to commence again through another rebirth in the constant turning of the wheel of sanmsaric suffering—until one achieves Awakening and the karma that binds one to the wheel of birth and death is finally overcome. Ideas such as these leave little room for narrative history, the implication of which is that the universe is purposeless and will, like everything caught in the field of space-time, eventually disappear. But the Christian narrative begins with a creation story and concludes with a final fulfillment, toward which all things and events in the universe—past, present, or future—are even now being lured.

Perhaps social activism that is specifically Christian is striving to build a world of peace and justice for human beings and the creatures of nature within the rough-and-tumble of historical events, which for Christian faith and practice is the locus, the place where God's continual action in the world is taking place. In this sense, history is the Christian counterpart of what Buddhists mean by dependent co-arising, because historical processes are interdependent processes in which all things and events are interrelated. Accordingly, the differences between Christian and Buddhist structures of social activism have more to do with the narrative assumptions underlying

23. Crossan, *The Dark Interval*, 101–7; also cited by Keenan, "Some Questions about the World," 183.

both traditions rather than differences between explicit doctrinal positions. The actual practice of Buddhist social engagement based on the doctrines of non-self, interdependence, impermanence, and compassion are not contrary to Christian experience. Nor do Christian social activist traditions based on faith and love in the struggle for justice for all persons and for nature contradict Buddhist traditions of social engagement. Christian social activism easily harmonizes with Buddhist teachings of interdependence and compassion with the Christian demand to love all in the struggle for justice with no strings attached, which I have described in another work as the practice of "loving/compassionate wisdom."[24]

THE QUESTION OF LIBERATION

Much of my dialogue with liberation theology has been with Christian and Buddhist women and men working to reform the patriarchal power structures of Christian and Buddhist tradition.[25] They have clarified for me that Buddhists and Christians need each other in the struggle not only for gender justice, but in the struggle for liberation itself. The question is, from what do human beings and seek liberation? What socially engaged Buddhists and Christian social activists tell us is that human beings seek liberation from suffering in many forms—from anxiety, from illness, from inferiority feelings, from grief, from fear of death, from social and economic injustice. What human beings seek may be healing, the elimination of agents of evil, access to power employed wisely and compassionately, the enhancement of status, increase of prosperity, the transformation of the social order, and ultimately the promise of life after death, resurrection from the grave, or freedom from continual rebirth in the realm of sanmsaric suffering and pain. Ultimate liberation is the topic of Christian soteriology and Buddhist teachings about Awakening. But the quest for liberation is not religion-specific so that dialogue with the world's religious traditions generally, and Buddhist-Christian dialogue particularly, provides resources for religious persons in their struggle for liberation.

The struggle for liberation from social injustice, gender injustice, and environmental injustice is systemic and global in nature. While the term "liberation" is not often used in Buddhist social activism, examples of Buddhist

24. Ingram, *Wrestling with God*, chap. 4.

25. For a fuller account of my views on Buddhist-Christian dialogue on these topics, see Ingram, *Wrestling with the Ox*, chaps. 5–8.

struggle for liberation abound: Dr. B. Ambedkar, who led millions of ex-untouchable Hindus to Buddhism—which gives no recognition to Hindu caste system; Dr. A. T. Ariyaratne, the founder of the Sarvodya Sramadana movement in Sri Lanka, whose goal is to establish new social structures that embody Buddhist values so that both individuals and society can achieve Awakening; the Dalai Lama's non-violent Tibetan liberation movement; Sulak Sivaraksi's "gadfly" attempts to lead the Thai government away from their participation in drug trafficking and the sex trade in South Asia; the Won Buddhist movement of South Korea, the Nichiren Buddhist movements of Rissho Koseikai and Soka Gakkai in Japan, and the Fo Kuang Shan move-ment in Taiwan that work to eradicate the systemic sources of economic and social injustice in their countries.[26]

The term "liberation" in Christian liberation theology, according to Gustavo Gutierrez, has two interdependent meanings.[27] First, "liberation" refers to the aspirations of oppressed human beings and social classes. In this sense, "liberation" names a process of struggle that places oppressed human beings at odds with oppressive national, social, economic, and political sys-tems. Seen from this perspective, emphasis is placed on the systemic sources of injustice so that "liberation practice" (*praxis*) means struggling to overcome these systemic forces. Second, "liberation" assumes a particular understanding of history. Christian liberation thinkers, for example, tend to see history as a process in which human beings gradually assume conscious responsibility for their own individual and collective global future. The focus of this responsi-bility is reflection on the meaning and struggle for social and political changes that have occurred in the past and are occurring in the present. "Accurate and usable history," to borrow a theme from feminist thought, is a major source for the creative struggle to establish political and economic justice. It is such struggle that Christian liberation theologians identify as "practice."

Of course, what liberation practice means will be nuanced differently in Buddhist social engagement and Christian social activism. For Christians, the central image of liberation is the historical Jesus as the Christ who brings liberation to human beings not only from the bondage of sin and death, but also from the social, economic, and political sins of oppression. Similarly, the chief model for liberation for Theravada Buddhists is the enlightened prac-tice of Gautama the Buddha, and for Mahayana Buddhists, all buddhas and bodhisattvas. Awakening must engender compassionate action "skillfully"

26 See Queen and King, eds., *Engaged Buddhism*, chaps. 2, 4, 6, 8, and 10.

27. Gutierrez, *A Theology of Liberation*, 36.

applied (*upāya*) to help liberate all sentient beings from suffering. Since the suffering that human beings and other life forms undergo is institutionalized within the structures of economic and political institutions, a necessary part of Buddhist practice is non-violent struggle to liberate all sentient beings from institutionalized structures of violent exploitation. It is for this reason that the leaders of socially engaged Buddhist movements regard the practice of meditation as the foundation of social activism. However, Christian liberation theologians tend to regard disciplines such as contemplative prayer and liturgical practice as secondary to the struggle for justice. In this regard, socially active Christians in dialogue with Buddhists have gradually either appropriated Buddhist meditative practices or have been inspired to incorporate Christian contemplative practices into their social activism.

One of the more important forms of Buddhist-Christian socially engaged dialogue focuses on the liberation of women from patriarchal oppression. In a chapter of my book *Wrestling with the Ox*, I argued that the liberation of women is the foundation for establishing social justice, economic justice, racial justice, and environmental justice because these forms of injustice originate from patriarchal assumptions about reality and the way social organizations should be structured according to these assumptions.[28] Of course what "patriarchy" means is a critical question. The feminist scholars who have helped me most in this regard are Rita M. Goss, who is a fellow historian of religions and a practicing Buddhist, and Nancy R. Howell, who is a Christian philosophical process theologian.[29] So I will follow their leads.

Androcentrism and patriarchy usually go together in Buddhist and Christian feminist writing. Androcentrism is a mode of consciousness, a thought-form, a method of gathering information and classifying women's place in a male defined metaphysical view of reality. Andocentric thought assumes that men represent the normative ideal that defines the meaning of being human, while women are portrayed as somehow peripheral to this norm. It asserts that the structure of humanity has one defining center, so that masculinity is the sole model for humanity.[30] As a worldview androcentrism occurs in both masculine and feminine heads, so that patriarchy is the institutionalized expression of androcentrism, which means that patriarchy

28. Ingram, *Wrestling with the Ox*, chap. 7.

29. See Gross, *Buddhism after Patriarchy*; and Howell, *A Feminist Cosmology*. Also see Howell's essay, "Beyond a Feminist Cosmology."

30. Gross, *Buddhism after Patriarchy*, 125–30 and Howell, *A Feminist Cosmology*, chap. 1. Also see Ruether, *Sexism and God Talk*, chap. 1.

always expresses itself as a gender hierarchy that places men over women. Men control women, or at least like to think they do.

While androcentrism and patriarchy are institutionalized differently in different cultures and religions, the end result is always the oppression of women as well as social, economic, racial, and environmental oppression in general. Methodologically, this fact means that Buddhist and Christian feminist writers working within their respective traditions are, according to Gross, faced with working through a "quadruple Androcentrism" in order to find "an accurate and usable past for women" within the Buddhist or Christian tradition so that Buddhism and Christianity can be "reconstructed" without patriarchal assumptions. Otherwise, neither Buddhist nor Christian women have reason to participate in Buddhism or Christianity.

In this regard, Buddhist and Christian feminists in dialogue seem to agree on four points. First, whenever any religious tradition chooses to preserve which literature to keep and whose experiences to preserve in their historical records, it usually operates with a male-centered or androcentric set of values. Stories about men and the thought and practices of men are far more likely to be recorded than stories about what women did or said. Second, even when a religious tradition preserves significant records about women, later developments within a religious tradition tend to ignore these stories and stress stories about male heroes as models of practice and attainment. Third, most Western scholarship on the world's religions is androcentric and often agrees with the male-centered biases that are structurally part of particular religious traditions, often ignoring the few existing records about women. Finally, all contemporary forms of the world's religious traditions continue to maintain an unrelenting, ongoing androcentrism.

Accordingly, Buddhist and Christian feminists, in agreement with feminists in other religious traditions, are faced with working through this quadruple androcentrism in order to reconstruct Buddhist and Christian tradition by means of recovering an accurate and usable past that focuses on the pluralism of Buddhist and Christian women's experiences. "Accuracy" has to do with feminism as an academic methodology of historical investigation, while "usability" refers to the feminist agenda for the liberation of both women and men from patriarchy.[31] If Buddhist and Christian feminists cannot reconstruct an accurate and useful history of Buddhism or Christianity that includes women's experiences as a constructive element of Buddhism's or

31. See Bancroft, "Women in Buddhism"; and Keller, "Walls, Women and Intimations of Interconnection."

Christianity's history, there is no reason for Buddhists of Christian women to remain in their respective religious traditions. Such a reconstruction should be liberating for both men and women, but if not, Buddhist and Christian women and men should leave.

This means that accurate history must be usable history. Since all historical records and interpretations of the past are selections, historical understanding is never unbiased or neutral. So the main issue is *how* historians choose relevant data. Buddhist and Christian feminists usually recognize that history is written and rewritten to reinforce values and perspectives a community deems important since historians always seek pasts that are not only accurate but also useable. Consequently, Buddhist and Christian feminist writers seek historical models, mostly ignored in androcentric historiography, of events that empower, rather than disempower, women. So a usable past is important because a religious community constitutes itself by its collective memory of the normative past events it recalls and remembers. This is as necessary for Buddhists, for whom the past *is not* revelatory, as it is for Christians for whom the past *is* revelatory. Accuracy is particularly important when justice issues are involved. When historical records and interpretations ignore women, a community is telling itself something negative about women's potential and place within that community. So if Buddhist or Christian feminists can recover an accurate, usable past for women, Buddhist and Christian communities will be creatively transformed. Bringing the stories of Buddhist and Christian women into the collective memory of Buddhists and Christians liberates both Buddhist and Christian women and men who are shaped by the history of patriarchal oppression.

For example, early Buddhism—Buddhism in its first two hundred years—conceptualized the experience of Awakening as transcendent and refused to characterize it in either its doctrinal or meditational disciplines with reference to gender. Awakening is quite literally beyond gender distinctions, and its liberating attainment is available to both men and women. Yet early Buddhism reflected the patriarchal social structure of the culture of its birth. Monastic institutions were patriarchal organizations, and Buddhist lay disciples, both men and women, had to defer to male monastic authority.[32] Likewise, the earliest "Jesus sayings" in the three Synoptic Gospels portray Jesus as quite free from the patriarchal biases of first century Judaism. Gender bias is absent from his teachings about the kingdom of God, God's love for all human beings, his call for social justice, and God's preferential option for the

32. Gross, *Buddhism after Patriarchy*, 31–48.

poor and oppressed. His attitudes toward women as well as his understanding of God were utterly free from gender biases. Yet within thirty years after his death, patriarchal biases became an institutional part of Christian faith and practice as Christianity was transmitted and institutionalized into the Hellenistic world of the Roman Empire.[33]

But as important as accurate and usable history is in energizing the quest for liberation from patriarchal forms of oppression, this has little value in itself unless this history provides resources for addressing and ending male oppression of women. What is certain is that the actual history of women's oppression in all the religious traditions is bleak indeed, so bleak that one may wonder why *anyone* would bother to reconstruct any religious tradition's past to include an accurate and usable history of women's experience. Given the history of women's oppression, why should any woman knowingly choose to stay and fight the hard battle to creatively transform her religious tradition? Given Christian standards of love and justice and Buddhist standards of compassionate social engagement, is it not morally wrong for any human being to stay under such patriarchal conditions? For if reality, the way things and events really are, is a pluralistic, organic system of interrelationships that constantly form and inform the existence of every thing and event in space-time—as Whitehead believed, Buddhist philosophy and contemporary physics confirm, and the parables of the historical Jesus teach—women's oppression is simultaneously men's oppression, even if injury to women is more immediately evident. What happens to any thing or event in the universe affects and effects all things and events. Male oppression of women breaks interrelationships that are absolutely required for the fulfillment of both women's and men's lives. Suffering and injury imposed on any human being by any human community are simultaneously the suffering, oppression, and injury of all. For this reason alone, just as white racism oppresses both people of color and white oppressors, as Martin Luther King and Mahatma Gandhi noted, so patriarchal oppression of women, who constitute over half the human species, oppresses male oppressors.

Accordingly, the liberation of women from patriarchal forms of oppression is interdependent with humanity's liberation from social, political, and economic forms of oppression, since women are generally the most socially, politically, and economically exploited human beings in every culture and religious context. The liberation of women from patriarchy is also interde-

33. See Borg, *Meeting Jesus Again for the First Time*, chaps. 5–6; and Crossan, *The Historical Jesus*, chap. 12.

pendent with the liberation of the environment from human exploitation. The lesson of socially engaged Buddhist and Christian dialogue is this: to the degree that women achieve liberation from patriarchal oppression, to that degree do we all achieve social, political, and economic liberation; to that degree does the Earth itself achieve liberation from human oppression; to that degree is life itself liberated from the threat of human-caused environmental distinction.

CONCLUDING OBSERVATIONS

I shall conclude this chapter with three observations: (1) Buddhist traditions of ethics and social activism are not less fully evolved than Christian traditions of ethics and social activism. Nor are Buddhist traditions of social engagement more fully evolved than traditions of Christian social activism. Buddhist social engagement and Christian social activism merely rest on different narrative versions about the structure of existence. (2) The question of which tradition is more ethically and socially engaged is neither important nor interesting. This question, therefore, should not be the focus of contemporary Buddhist-Christian socially engaged dialogue. (3) Buddhists and Christians share the same planet and the same problems all human beings share: the necessity of being socially engaged with the systemic forces that endanger the human community along with all life on planet Earth. The oppression of women, consumerism, poverty, political oppression, racism, and ecological degradation of the environment are so serious in their present scope that conceptual differences between Buddhist and Christian religious teachings and practices, while theologically and philosophically interesting, pale to insignificance. Or to paraphrase what the Buddha is reported to have said when asked to resolve unsolvable philosophical puzzles, resolving doctrinal differences between Buddhism and Christianity "is not conducive to Awakening." Nor is it conducive to Christian experience of God's saving grace.

5

Buddhist-Christian Interior Dialogue

If participants in Buddhist-Christian interior dialogue are to be believed, in the common struggle for liberation Christians and Buddhists share an experiential common ground or referent that enables them to hear one another and be mutually transformed in the process. Interior dialogue concentrates on participating in Christian and Buddhist spiritual practices and techniques coupled with reflection on the resulting experiences. The main concerns of interior dialogue arise directly out of the practice traditions of both traditions.

Of course, the meaning of "practice" (*praxis*) in the context of interior dialogue requires clarification. Normally, whenever we hear the word "practice," the meaning we are likely to call to mind is its popular instrumental meaning: practice names something opposed to theory. In this sense theory and theoretical knowledge are ends in themselves, while "practice is a means to achieve a theoretical end outside itself."[1] Practice most often appears as something one does to achieve a theoretically formulated goal that one has not yet achieved, as in practicing the piano to achieve skilled concert-level performance. Or as athletes practice tennis to win matches and tournaments, so Buddhists practice meditation to achieve Awakening and Carmelite nuns practice contemplative prayer to achieve union with Christ the Bridegroom. So religious practices are normally understood as instrumental means to achieve a theoretical end separate from practice. But this common instrumentalist view of practice is an oversimplification. As John C. Maraldo writes: "This is the fact that theory, by way of its Latin translation, has been associated

---

1. What follows is based on Maraldo's essay on practice, "The Hermeneutic of Practice in Dogen and Francis of Assisi."

with contemplation and the purely contemplative, that is, apolitical life—the life later associated with religious meditation. Thus we are confronted with a view which would take the theoretical life paradoxically as the life of religious practice."[2] In other words, practice and attainment of a theoretically formulated end are not separate in the experience of religious persons. "Practice *is* attainment"; attainment *is* practice. Practice and attainment are non-dual.

It is this non-instrumental meaning of practice that describes what religious persons actually experience when they practice their religious faith. Any activity that requires practice to be performed efficiently can serve as an illustration. One can, for example, think of learning to play the piano, or learning a foreign language, or learning a martial art, or performing Japanese tea ceremony, or flower arranging. To say that mastery of these arts takes practice means that repeated effort and concentration are absolute requirements in the process of learning. Such activities are daily performances practiced for no other goal than their performance. So when a tea master conducts a tea ceremony, she is performing the same kind of activity when she was a novice beginning her study of this art. For her, there is no difference between practice and skilled performance. Her performance is her practice; her practice is her performance. As a master of her art, she experiences no duality between her practice and her performance; no gaps exist between what she wills to do and what she does.

Such non-duality between practice and attainment is experientially true for the masters of any art or discipline demanding skilled performance. It is only novices who experience a gap between practice and skilled performance. For them, practice is something one does to achieve an end one desires, but has not yet attained. Thus a novice practices to attain skilled performance. But for the master, there is never a time when practice is not skilled attainment or skilled performance not practice. However, even for a novice, practice is attainment even though this might not be perceived as so.

It is this non-instrumental sense of practice that is emphasized in Christian contemplative and Buddhist meditative forms of religious discipline. Thus novices at the beginning stages of religious practice often experience a separation between their performance and their theoretically formulated attainment. Novice Buddhist monks and nuns, for example, practice their disciplines as an instrumental means to achieve Awakening. They perceive themselves as unawakened and practice to become Awakened. But for Awakened ones, practice is awakened attainment; attainment is awakened practice. Yet for

2. Ibid., 55.

novices, practice is attainment as well, only they do not ususaaly perceive that this is so. Or as the Soto Zen master Dogen once instructed the monks under care: "The Dharma is amply present in every person, but unless one practices, it is not manifested, unless there is realization, it is not attained . . . As it is already realization in practice, realization is endless; as sitting in practice is realization, practice is beginningless."[3]

Similarly, Christian contemplative practices are also non-instrumental. Maraldo illustrates this with the example of the contemplative practice of Francis Assisi. As Francis understood the prologue of the Gospel of John, Christ is present in all persons, so for Francis practice had four interrelated dimensions: (1) it is learned by following a normative Rule with specific injunctions; (2) it is actualized in ordinary, everyday actions and situations; (3) it is persistently and consistently applied; and (4) it is itself the proclamation of the "gospel life"—living in obedience and chastity, without property, in order to imitate the practices of Christ.[4] In other words, practice—contemplative prayer, the life of poverty, labor on behalf of others—*is* the gospel life; the gospel life *is* practice. Practice and attainment are non-dual.

Since spiritual and monastic disciplines continue to energize Catholic experience, while monasticism and disciplines such as contemplative prayer have, since Luther's time, been viewed as forms of "works righteousness" and consequently de-emphasized in Protestant tradition, Roman Catholics have been more open to interior dialogue with Buddhists. While a number of Catholic monks, nuns, and laity are interested in this form of dialogue with Buddhism, Thomas Merton's encounter with the Dalai Lama and other Tibetan monks, Thai Buddhists monks, and Zen teachers still serves as a paradigm for other Catholic and some Protestant thinkers.

Merton's specific interest in Buddhism evolved out of his frustration with the state of Catholic monasticism as he had experienced it as a Trappist. Toward the end of his life, he had reached the conclusion that Christian monastic traditions should be reformed by means of dialogue with Buddhist monks and nuns through the mutual participation and sharing of Christian-Buddhist meditative techniques and experiences.[5] The purpose of "contemplative dialogue," as he referred to what is now called "interior dialogue," is to discover whether there exist similarities and analogies in Christian and Buddhist experience in spite of the doctrinal differences in Christian and

3. Abe and Wadell, trans., "Dogen's *Bendowa*," 129.

4. Maraldo, "The Hermeneutics of Practice in Dogen and Francis of Assisi," 58.

5. Merton, "Monastic Experience and East-West Dialogue," 309–25.

Buddhist thought. He came to the conclusion that while doctrinal differences will always differentiate Christian and Buddhist tradition, doctrinal differences do not invalidate the existential similarities of the experiences engendered by Christian and Buddhist monastic disciplines like contemplative prayer and meditation. He grew to believe that the realities experientially discovered by both Buddhists and Christians is beyond the power of doctrine to delimit and specify in any complete way.[6]

In this regard, Raimundo Panikkar, in *The Silence of God, the Answer of the Buddha*, explored the conceptual incommensurability between Christian theism and Buddhist non-theism as a means of helping Christians search for new meanings of God beyond the limits of the traditional categories of Euro-American theological tradition. Unlike Cobb's primarily conceptual dialogue with Buddhism, the stress of Panikkar's encounter with Buddhism combines interior dialogue with conceptual dialogue. This interest reflects Pannikar's training as a Jesuit. As a Jesuit schooled in the traditions of Catholic monastic and mystical theology, his intention is to help Christians experience, as well as rationally understand, that the object of Christian faith is a reality that is beyond the boundaries of theological thought, including Christian and Buddhist doctrines. Accordingly, Christians need to hear the "answer of the Buddha": the ultimate reality to which the Buddha awoke as non-personal and beyond language and symbol. Appropriating the Buddha's answer becomes in Panikkar's thought a method of entering the "silence that is the reality of God" beyond the limitations of doctrinal description, even those of Christian theology.[7]

"Entering the silence," as Merton phrased it, has always been the goal of Catholic monastic practice and is the heart of Christian mystical theology, according to which doctrines are symbolic pointers, not literal descriptions. Cling to a doctrine *about* God, one only has a doctrine *about* God; comprehend that doctrines are symbolic pointers to a reality beyond the definitions of doctrine, one has a means of entering the silence that is God beyond anything theological reflection can imagine God to be or not to be.

Rubin Habito develops Panikkar's arguments further. Among Catholic Christians presently engaged with Buddhism, Habito is unique in that (1) he trained in Zen meditation under Yamada Koun Roshi (1907–1989) and

---

6. Merton, "Marxism and Monastic Disciplines," 332–42. Also see Cunningham, *Thomas Merton and the Monastic Vision*, 155–82.

7. Montaldo, ed., *Entering the Silence*; and Panikkar, *The Silence of God, the Answer of the Buddha*, chap. 10.

received Yamada Roshi's "seal of approval" (*inko*) as his Dharma heir during his years in Japan as a Jesuit, and (2) he is interested in both interior and conceptual dialogue with Buddhism. Accordingly, the focus of Habito's theological encounter with Buddhism is his interior dialogue with Zen Buddhist traditions of practice, which he has incorporated into his particular form of contemplative prayer, along with the reformulation of Christian theological categories in light of his interior dialogue with Buddhism. In this, he is rooted in Roman Catholic traditions of interior dialogue with Buddhism that include Philip Johnston, Thomas Merton, and Thomas Keating.[8]

The central theological question Habito brings to dialogue with Buddhism centers on the question of liberation. Since both Christian and Buddhist practices are methods of experiencing liberation, Habito is interested in the core of Buddhist and Christian identity, symbolized by the Buddha's Awakening experience under the Tree of Awakening and Jesus as the Christ hanging from the cross.

For example, in an essay titled "The Resurrection of the Dead and Life Everlasting: From a Futuristic to a Realized Christianity," Habito points to an article in the Apostle's Creed—"I believe in . . . the resurrection of the body and the life everlasting"—as the source for what he perceives is the interplay between the "future outlook" and, borrowing a phrase from Zen Buddhist teaching, the "realized outlook" of Christian experience. While both outlooks are interdependent and presuppose faith as trust in the promise of eternal life made manifest in the historical Jesus' life, death, and resurrection (the future aspect), he argues that the resurrection of the body and life everlasting are simultaneously a present reality open to anyone who accepts Christ here and now (the realized aspect). Hence Christian faith's realized aspect entails the experience of eternal life and resurrection in the here-and-now moment of the experience of faith. Zen's stress on experiencing the liberating insight of Awakening in the here-and-now moment of experience can help Christians appreciate the realized aspect of the Christian experience of liberation more fully. Habito's biblical support for this conclusion is the last judgment scene in Matthew 23:31–46, which proclaims that faith in Jesus as the Christ entails a way of life open to the needs of one's neighbors, which is the gate to a

8. Cf. Johnston, *Silent Music*; Thomas Keating, *Invitation to Love*; Merton, *Mystics and Zen Masters*; and Merton, *The Asian Journal of Thomas Merton*, 211–56, 297–304, 309–17.

future eternal life experienced in a realized moment of awakened experience in the here-and-now.[9]

THE GETHSEMANI ENCOUNTER

In 1978, ten years after Merton's death, two Catholic dialogue commissions were created: the Monastic Interreligious Dialogue (MID) in North America and the Dialogue Inter-Monastic (DIM) in Europe. From these two commissions grew the Spiritual Exchange in Europe and since 1981 the Monastic Hospitality Program in North America, programs in which Buddhist monks and nuns spent time living in Christian monasteries in the West, while Christian monastic's were guests of Zen and Tibetan monasteries in the East. Prior to the Parliament of the World's Religions in 1993, Fr. Julian von Duerbeck, OSB, and Br. Wayne Teasdale proposed that the MID host an interfaith dialogue session at the Parliament with the Dalai Lama and other Buddhist leaders. It was the Dalai Lama who suggested that that the monastic dialogue be continued at Thomas Merton's monastery at Gethsemani. This is the background for the Gethsemani Encounter, the first meeting of which was the evening of July 22, 1996, at Gethsemani Abby in Trappist, Kentucky. The encounter lasted five days and included twenty-five invited Buddhist monks and nuns and twenty-five Catholic monks and nuns plus a few Protestants.

The interior dialogue of the participants in the Gethsemani Encounter focused on the "spiritual unity" underlying the doctrinal plurality of the world's religious traditions, here illustrated by the relation between Buddhist and Christian monastic practices and their respective doctrinal differences. For example, according to the Dalai Lama, the source of this spiritual unity is an Absolute Reality experienced and named differently through the practice of Buddhist meditative disciplines and Christian contemplative disciplines. As summarized by the Dalai Lama:

> Now, it is also quite clear that different religious traditions—in spite of having different philosophies and viewpoints—all have great potential to help humanity by promoting human happiness and satisfaction. As a matter of fact, it is quite clear that given the vast array of humanity—of so many different kinds of people with different mental dispositions—we need, and so it is far better to have, a variety of religious traditions. Religions are like medicine in

9. See Habito, *Healing Breath*; and Habito, "The Resurrection of the Dead, and Life Everlasting."

that the important thing is to cure human suffering. In the practice of medicine it is not a question of how expensive the medicine is; what is important is to cure the illness in a particular patient. Similarly, you see there are a variety of religions with their different philosophies and traditions and the aim and purpose of each is to cure the pains and unhappiness of the human mind. Here too, it is not a question of which religion is superior as such. The question is, which will better cure a particular person.[10]

Accordingly, interior dialogue "is not necessarily done in order to a[dopt the spiritual practices of other traditions] to ourselves, but in order to increase our opportunities for mutual respect. Sometimes too, we encounter something in another tradition that helps us better appreciate something in our own."[11]

The Dalai Lama's understanding of this spiritual unity presupposes the categories of Madhyamika philosophy's distinction between relative truth and Absolute Truth. Thus the sources of religious pluralism lay in the distinctive secondary conceptual traditions of each tradition—their worldviews, theologies, and doctrines. These are relative truths. But the spiritual practices of the particular world religions, including Buddhism and Christianity, point to the Absolute Truth of which conceptualized doctrines are merely secondary pointers—an Absolute Truth named differently in each religious tradition. In Mahayana Buddhism, this Absolute Truth is named Emptying, in Theravada Buddhism it is named the Dharma, and in Christian experience it is named God manifested in the Logos incarnated in the historical Jesus as the Christ.

Similarly, in his description of contemplative prayer as a form of "mindfulness," Pierre-François de Béthune, OSB, observes: "As of today, new encounters with the realities of our contemporary world challenge the faithful to renew the prayerful practice of their faith in Christ. One of the major encounters in the course of recent years is indeed the discovery made by Christians of the spiritual practices elaborated in Hinduism, Buddhism, and other religions. This encounter is a new opportunity for an ever more lively practice of Christian prayer."[12] Therefore,

with a heart enlarged by the love of God that embraces all of creation, he or she is spontaneously in communion with all those who suffer and all those who follow the spiritual life,, *whatever their religion*. Ultimately, the prayer of the Holy Spirit that brings

10. Tenzin, "Harmony, Dialogue, and Meditation," 47.

11. Tenzin, "Foreword," x.

12. De Béthune, "Prayer as Path," 82.

us into this communion is that all humanity and even the whole creation which, as St. Paul says, groans and travails in pain (Rom 8:26). Conversely, the opportunity to meet other fellow pilgrims stimulates us to deepen our prayer.[13]

According to the participants at Gethsemani, specific meditative and contemplative prayer techniques lead Buddhists and Christian practitioners to a unitive experience of an Absolute Reality that both transcends and is simultaneously immanent within all things and events at every moment of space-time. This experience, known in Christian mystical theology as "apophatic" experience, is unitary in structure for both Buddhists and Christians. During such experience, subject-object differentiations utterly drop away from consciousness so that reality, meaning the way things really are in contrast to the way our egos might want things to be, is apprehended without doctrinal conceptualities. The Buddhist and Christian participants also agreed that such apprehension engenders compassionate wisdom through which the monk or nun is empowered to creatively engage the sources of human suffering at work in the world. In other words, monastic practices like meditation in its plurality of forms and centering prayer in its plurality of forms engenders structurally similar experiences for Buddhist and Christians in spite of the conceptual differences in the Buddhist and Christian doctrines that guide the practice of meditation and centering prayer.

The Dalai Lama's views on this point are expressive of the views of most Theravada and Mahayana monks and nuns engaged in interior dialogue with Christian contemplatives. The doctrinal formulations of the Buddhist worldview are forms of *upāya* or "skillful method" or "teaching" that point persons to the experience of Awakening. But the truth to which doctrines symbolically point transcends all conceptual pointers. They are, according to the Dalai Lama's Madhyamika doctrinal point of view, secondary truths. Clinging to secondary truths is a fundamental cause of suffering for all sentient beings. And in point of fact, religious persons clinging to religious doctrines have caused much human and environmental suffering. Or to appropriate a well-known Zen Buddhist formulation of this principle, one should never "stink" of Buddhism or Christianity.

Nevertheless, Buddhist doctrines guide the practice of meditation in all schools of Buddhism. The purpose of Buddhist meditation is to purify the mind of mental distortions caused by clinging to permanence so that one

13. Ibid., 87–88, emphasis added.

can apprehend the "Emptiness" (*śūnyatā*) of things and events and thereby not cling to delusions, particularly the delusion of permanent selfhood. Accomplishing this requires a powerfully concentrated mind. While there exists a plurality of meditative disciplines, five common assumptions guide Buddhist practice traditions.

- Since the development of mindfulness requires the avoidance of negative activities, ethics is the foundation for techniques of meditation.

- Meditation can be practiced by concentrating on just one object—this is called "stabilizing meditation" in Tibetan Buddhism.

- Meditation can be analytical, as in Theravada "calming" (*samatha*) and "insight" (*vipassanā*) meditation, through which the reasons and supporting attitudes and emotions, both positive and negative, can be apprehended and replaced by non-egotistic emotions like compassion that engenders the apprehension of universal interdependence.

- Meditation may also be a reflection on the various levels of a spiritual path.

- Meditation may involve visualization techniques, chanting mantras, or simply focusing on one's breathing or a *koan*.

In other words, what "meditation" names is a group of mental techniques meant to experientially confirm the truth of Buddhism's worldview and defining doctrines.

Likewise, the goal of Christian contemplative practices of centering prayer and *lectio divina* ("divine reading") is experiential confirmation of the truth of Christian teachings about God as incarnated in the life, death, and resurrection of the historical Jesus. In comparing the goals of Buddhist meditation and Christian contemplative practice, Donald Mitchell writes: "in reading the description of the qualities of a person who abides in *Nibbana*, namely, compassion, loving kindness, sympathetic joy, and equanimity—one recognized the qualities of a person who abides in the Kingdom of God. On the other hand, while *Nibbana* is primarily a state of consciousness, when we Christians gaze into the heart of our supreme refuge with the 'mind of Christ,' we find a personal God who is 'love.'"[14]

Historically, some Christian contemplatives have had apophatic experiences that seem structurally similar to Buddhist experiences of Awakening

14. Mitchell, "God, Creation, and the Spiritual Life," 28.

in the sense that the distinctions of doctrine become secondary truths. Historically, many of these contemplatives have been judged to be heretical, or at least verging on heresy. My favorite mystical theologian, Marguerite Porete, will serve as an illustration. Marguerite belonged to a distinguished line of thirteenth-century beguine mystical writers that included Mechthild of Magdeburg and Hadewijch of Antwerp. She had written a book—*The Mirror of Simple Souls*—that was condemned and burned in her presence at Valenciennes by Guy II, Bishop of Cambria, in 1306. She was later accused of circulating the *Mirror* after its condemnation and was brought before Guy's successor, Philippe of Marigny, who turned her over to the inquisitor of Haute Loraine. Eventually, she was handed over to the Dominican inquisitor of Paris, Guillaume Humbert.

Marguerite refused to cooperate with the proceedings against her, to testify, or to take the formal oath required of persons charged with heresy. So without her testimony, Humbert submitted a list of articles from the *Mirror* to twenty-one regents of the University of Paris, who declared fifteen heretical. A panel of canon lawyers then handed her over to the provost of Paris to be burned along with a converted Jew who was charged with relapse. In 1309, Guiard de Cressonessart, who called himself the "Angel of Philadelphia," intervened on Marguerite's behalf, and he too was arrested and ordered to renounce his teachings. Unlike Marguerite, the Angel of Philadelphia recanted and was condemned to life imprisonment. Within a few years of her burning,[15] Marguerite's name was being associated with a movement called "the heresy of the free spirit" and her *Mirror* was influencing the development of Meister Eckhart's mystical theology, portions of whose sermons were condemned as heretical for reasons similar to Marguerite's condemnation. Unlike Marguerite, however, Eckhart was not arrested, tortured, and burned at the stake.[16]

15. Marguerite's trial, condemnation, and execution were, according to Bernard McGinn, "a critical moment in the history of Christian mysticism, and one equivalent to the execution of Al-Hallaj in the story of Islamic mysticism. Marguerite is the first documented case of an execution for mystical heresy in Western Christianity . . . Unfortunately, it was not to be the last. Her death was not just an individual tragedy; it also provided critical ammunition for an ongoing struggle between the mystical and the institutional elements of Christianity that has continued almost down to the present day." McGinn, *The Flowering of Mysticism*, 244.

16. For a discussion of Marguerite's influence on Meister Eckhart's mystical theology, see Lichtmann, "Marguerite Porete and Meister Eckhart"; Hollywood, "Suffering Transformed"; and Michel Sells, "The Pseudo-Woman and the Meister."

Marguerite wrote the *Mirror* as a dramatic allegory in which the five characters—Lady Love (*Dame Amour*), Annihilated Soul (*L'Ame Anneantie*), Reason (*Raison*), FarNear (*Loingprès*) and High Courtesy (*Pure Courtoise*)—engage in an extended discussion on love and theology. The text brings together the paradoxes of mystical theology and the troubadour tradition of courtly love into a mystical language of rapture. The result is an apophasis of desire.

The high point of the drama occurs when Reason—identified with the Aristotelian epistemology of the schools and their theologians—is so perplexed by the paradoxes of Lady Love that Reason dies. The context of the dialogue that leads to Reason's death is a seven-tiered cosmos of mystical stations, the fifth and sixth of which are the center of the *Mirror's* interest, with the seventh station being beyond all words and associated by Lady Love with the afterlife.

Early in the *Mirror*, Marguerite describes the "simple soul" as a soul in union with God whose will is annihilated in and by God's love. Such a soul is (1) saved by faith without works, (2) exists only in love, (3) does nothing for God, (4) leaves nothing for God to do, (5) one to whom nothing can be taught, (6) from whom nothing can be taken or given, and (7) has no will.[17] Each of these items is a deliberate provocation of Reason and the medieval church's understanding of the way of salvation. The teachings of what Marguerite calls "Holy Church the Little" (the "secondary truths" of church doctrine) can be superseded only by the shock to Reason that this description of the liberated soul in union with God entails. Reason, jolted into attention, is driven to demand from Lady Love an explanation—much like the inquisitors who interrogated Marguerite.

Lady Love then describes the seven-stage process whereby the soul is led to union with God.[18] These stages include the ascetic, churchly, and contemplative practices advocated by the majority of thirteenth-century religious and semi-religious persons. In her description of the lower stages, Marguerite rejected those forms of ascetic, ecstatic, and mystical piety particularly associated with women.[19] For the soul, she writes, must pass through seven stages, each initiated by God's grace and each marked by three deaths: the death of sin, the death of nature, and the death of the spirit. Subsequent to each death

17. Porete, *The Mirror of Simple Souls*, 82–83.

18. The most detailed description of these stages is found in ibid., chap. 118.

19. Hollywood, *The Soul as Virgin Wife*, 97–103. Also see Jo Ann McNamara, "The Rhetoric of Orthodoxy."

are two stages, one characterized by complacency and the other by a sense of dissatisfaction that leads to the next death.

The soul enters stage one after the initial death to sin, at which point the soul is given divine grace and thereby freed from mortal sin, which pushes the soul to follow the two-fold commandment to love God and the soul's neighbor. When this minimal Christian life seems inadequate, the soul is drawn into stage two. Here, the soul abandons all riches and honors in order to follow the evangelical counsel of perfection, of which Christ is the example in medieval theology. This initiates the soul's death to nature and leads to stage three. Now the soul possesses an abundance of love and desires to do good works, which paradoxically leads the soul to give up all external works in order to be capable of greater love for God. This is the life of contemplation, ascetic piety, poverty, fasts, prayers, devotions, and martyrdoms—in other words, monasticism.

Marguerite thought most of her contemporaries were stuck on stage three and she describes them as "lost souls" stuck in "Holy Church the Little." Lost souls, according to her, are incapable of attaining freedom because of their refusal to see that asceticism, contemplation, and spiritual delight do not represent the soul's highest perfection because such practices—based on self-willed works—merely serve to absent the soul from God. But rather than taking the divine absence as an intrinsic part of union with God, lost souls attempt to elicit experiences of divine sweetness through suffering, asceticism, and internal contemplative works. Such souls, she says, are "merchants" who believe that one can barter with God.

God, however, draws some souls into stage four, where the first steps toward simplicity are experienced. The soul now has become bewildered. That is, although still "merchants" and "servants" and still possessed of will and works, souls at this stage are no longer lost because they recognize that bewilderment is better than nothing. This recognition leads to renunciation of the will, which is stage five. Here, the soul recognizes its previous self-deceptions, which in turn engenders fleeting experiences of the utter and complete transparency of the soul in its union with God. This marks the death of the spirit, which is twofold, involving both the death of reason and the death of will. This experience pushes the soul into stage six, union with God, which in turn is completed at stage seven when the soul departs the body at death to be permanently in union with God—a stage beyond description, but of which the soul catches imperfect glimpses at stage six.

For our purposes, two ingredients of this framework of spiritual progress are important to understand. First, Marguerite's description of the three
kinds of death are transitions which give birth successively to three "higher"
forms of life as they move the soul toward spiritual perfection. Death to sin
gives birth to the life of grace in stage one. Here, one begins with the commandments of the church and the help of God, who commands that one
love God with all of one's strength, mind, and heart and one's neighbor as
one's self. The life of grace is the life of ordinary believers. Death to nature
gives birth to the life of the spirit, meaning the attempt to follow the counsels
of evangelical perfection. This is life lived in obedience guided by reason.
Death to the spirit gives birth to the divine life. The spirit must die because
it is filled with will. Even though will in the life of the spirit is spiritual, it
is still will. The death of the spirit and the departure of will in stage five are
absolutely necessary for the birth of stage six. All rudiments of the soul's own
will must be annihilated by the divine will, which then, at stage six, becomes
the soul's will. In this state the soul wills nothing; *God's will wills the willing
of the annihilated soul*. That is, between the soul's will—we might say "self" in
contemporary speech—and God's will or self, *there exists no ontological duality*. Or in Marguerite's language, what takes place at stage six is an "exchange
of wills,"[20] which Michael Sells describes as an "apophasis of desire": "The
apophasis of desire includes the admonition to give nature all that it desires,
but that admonition applies to the annihilated soul in which nature and will
and spirit have died. After the death of the will, the soul no longer needs to
work contrary to her will because the soul is no longer the doer or the worker,
but rather the deity works in her."[21]

Marguerite's *Mirror* is not representative of Christian understanding
of the relation between theological reflection and contemplative experience,
either in her time or in contemporary Catholic contemplative theology.
Certainly, nothing similar to her interpretation of the mystical experience of
unity with God occurred among the Christian participants in the Gethsemani
Encounter. For most Christian contemplatives, in Marguerite's time or today,
the christological statements of the creeds of the church are normative in the
sense that any contemplative experience that cannot be formulated in the
categories of orthodox doctrinal statements about the historical Jesus as the
Christ would not be regarded as authentically Christian, even though they
might be recognized as similar to Buddhist experience. Indeed, the Christian

20. Porete, *The Mirror of Simple Souls*, 166.

21. Sells, "The Pseudo-Woman and the Meister," 114.

monks, nuns, and laypersons at Gethsemani seemed to have dialogically engaged Buddhist monks, nuns and laity through the inclusive theological filter of Rahner's "anonymous Christianity."

That is, to the degree that Buddhist Awakening experience seemed structurally similar to Christian contemplative experience of union with God, to that degree could it be affirmed that Christians and Buddhist had experienced a similar reality named differently. But the way in which Buddhist monastics relate the experience of Awakening to doctrinal statements *about* Awakening is also inclusive in this sense. To the degree that Christian contemplative experience seems similar to Buddhist meditative experience, and vice versa, to that degree there are enough structural similarities that Buddhists can affirm the reality of Christian apprehensions of a common reality that unifies both Buddhists and Christians, which is the point of each of the Dalai Lama's talks at the Gethsemani Encounter.

What Buddhists and Christians engaged in interior dialogue tell us is that the reality they experience and speak about transcends linguistic construction. Whether Buddhist or Christian, the structure of such experience is best described as "apophatic." Apophatic mysticism always generates a linguistic paradox. Here is St. Augustine's reflection on the paradox of mystical discourse:

> Have we spoken or announced anything worthy of God? Rather I feel that I have done nothing but wish to speak: If I have spoken, I have not said what I wish to say. Whence do I know this, except because God is ineffable? If what I said were ineffable, it would not be said. And for this reason God should not be said to be ineffable, for when this is said something is said. And a contradiction in terms is created, since if that is ineffable which cannot be spoken, then that is not ineffable which can be called ineffable. The contradiction is to be passed over in silence rather than resolved verbally. For God, although nothing worthy may be spoken of him, has accepted the tribute of human voice and wished us to take joy in praising him with our words.[22]

Unlike St. Augustine, perhaps foolishly, I am not willing silently to pass over the paradox of Buddhist and Christian talk about their unitive experiences, though I agree that this paradox cannot be resolved. If it could, theologians, philosophers, and historians of religions could get on with their jobs with the aplomb of bricklayers. Certainly Buddhists and Christians do not

---

22. Augustine, *On Christian Doctrine*, book 1, chaps. 6, 10–11.

silently pass over the linguistic paradoxes engendered by their talk about an ineffable ultimate reality.

What is going on here? To answer this question, a brief reflection on mystical discourse is in order. First, it is not possible to completely distinguish between apophatic mystical experiences and their theological or philosophical interpretations in any absolute way. For in most cases, mystical theory precedes and guides the mystic's whole way of life and directs his or her "practice" (*praxis*). This is why Mahayana Buddhist nuns do not normally interpret their experiences of non-duality with the Buddha Nature as union with the Christ the Bridegroom, nor do Carmelite nuns usually interpret their experiences of union with Christ the Bridegroom as non-duality with the Empty Buddha Nature in, with, and under all things and events at every moment of space-time. Theory—that is, theology, and, in non-Western traditions of mysticism, philosophy—"is not some form of epiphenomenon, a shell that can be peeled off to reveal the real thing."[23] In this regard, three points require clarification.

First, while apophatic experiences of union are characterized by a common structure within whatever cultural and religious context they occur, Buddhist and Christian experience of union with a transcendent and immanent reality are not identical. This is so because part of a meditator's or contemplative's experience is the *preparation undergone before the experience occurs* and *the interpretation of the experience after it occurs*. This fact constitutes part of the evidence I cited in chapter 1 in support of the pluralist hypothesis. But as the neurosciences are now demonstrating, given the common neurological structure of the human brain and central nervous system that has been evolving among *homo sapiens* for thirty-five to forty thousand years, it can be reasonably argued even on biological grounds that unitive mystical *experience* occurring across different religious traditions exhibits a common structure that is not culturally or religiously specific, even as *how* mystics interpret the *meaning* these experiences *is* culturally and religiously specific. This too is evidence that I believe supports the pluralist hypothesis. The neurological foundation of contemplative experience is the topic of the following section.

Second, what I am calling Buddhist and Christian mystical experience is one element of Buddhist and Christian experience. No mystics have ever believed in or practiced something called "mysticism." They believed in or practiced Christianity, Judaism, Islam, Buddhism, Hinduism, or Taoism. So "mysticism" names a particular religious process. Although the goal of

23. McGinn, *Foundations of Mysticism*, xiii–xiv.

mystical theory and practice may be conceived as a particular kind of unitive encounter between God and humanity or the experience of Awakening, "everything that leads up to and prepares the mystic for the encounter, as well as all that flows from it for the life of the mystic in the belief of the community, is also mystical, even in a secondary sense."[24]

Third, mysticism is an attempt to experience and express direct consciousness of the presence of God (in Christian tradition) or of a non-personal ultimate reality (in Buddhist tradition). Sometimes this presence is expressed as "union" or "oneness," which in Western scholarship is called "apophatic mysticism." Sometimes mystical experience is not a matter of union—for most theistic mystics the direct experience of God's presence does not, as it did for Marguerite, involve ontological union with God, which in Western scholarship is designated "cataphatic mysticism." So the conceptual foundations of a religious tradition are part of its beliefs and practices that concern the preparation *for*, consciousness *of*, and reaction *to* the immediate or direct presence of God—in Christianity, Judaism, Islam, or theistic forms of Hinduism—or the Brahman of Hindu Advaita Vedanta, Sunyata of Mahayana Buddhism, or the Tao of Chinese religion.[25]

Finally, mysticism as a religious phenomenon is as pluralistic as the religious traditions that house meditative and contemplative practices and experiences. Yet there is one non-tradition specific thing about which all actual mystics seem to agree: apophatic mystical experience defies verbalization and conceptualization because it is utterly empty of content. Accordingly, it can only be publicly presented indirectly, practically, poetically, by a series of verbal strategies in which language is used not so much informationally as transformationally; that is, not to convey a content but to assist the hearer or reader to hope for or to achieve the same contentless consciousness.

So the paradoxes inherent within apophatic mystical discourse—whatever their cultural and religious context—are not merely apparent contradictions. The contradictions and paradoxes are real, but not irrational, illogical, or incoherent. For the apophatic mystical writer, the logical rule of non-contradiction functions for object entities. But when the subject of discourse is a non-object and a no-thing, it is not illogical when the logical rules of ordinary discourse are superseded. Certainly, apophatic mystical discourse is not the only discourse that cannot directly name its object. For example, the reason many mystics choose poetry for their mode of expression has to do

24. Ibid., xvi.
25. Ibid.

with the ways in which poetry tests and subverts ordinary discursive language. Poets and mystics both overcome the limits of discursive language because poetry, drama—most any art form—risks being trivialized when its meaning is defined or paraphrased discursively, as anyone knows who needs to have the humor of a joke explained.

THE NEUROLOGICAL FOUNDATIONS OF CONTEMPLATIVE EXPERIENCE[26]

As noted in chapter 3, the collection of disciplines comprising the neurosciences has special relevance for Buddhist and Christian monastic and contemplative practice. The reasons are obvious. The theoretical perspective and research of the cognitive sciences will directly affect how we think about the human person, from the nature of consciousness, to issues of freedom, to religious experience, to how we think about ourselves within the larger context of the natural world. This is so because the human mind appears connected to other minds through culture, to our relation to other animals, and to a common evolutionary past. For Christians, obviously, the cognitive sciences will constrain how one thinks about and experiences God and God's relation to the world since Christians often think of God as a mind or a person.

Certainly, God is not an issue for Buddhists. Nevertheless the neurosciences require both Buddhists and Christians to rethink their worldviews and practice traditions. The nature of consciousness and mind are important areas of research and discussion, not only for the cognitive sciences but also for Buddhist doctrinal traditions and meditative practice, as well as for Christian theology and the practice of centering prayer. In Christian theology, the "signs of the spirit" in humanity—whether in the three-part anthropology of the New Testament (*sarx, psyche, pneuma*, or "flesh, soul, spirit") or in more dualistic accounts that have separated the mind and body in Western thought since René Descartes—have long been taken as proof of God's existence and as evidence of the *imago Dei* in humanity. The doctrine that human beings are "images of God" has, in turn, been a theological justification for sharply segregating human beings from all other living beings, as well as for patriarchal exploitation of nature and male oppression of females. While philosophical dualism has not been a metaphysical assumption of Buddhist teaching and practice, understanding the nature of self-awareness—mental experiences

26. For a fuller account of Buddhist and Christian encounter with the neurological sciences, see Ingram, *Buddhist-Christian Dialogue in an Age of Science*, chap. 5.

such as anger, hope, happiness, suffering, release from suffering, and the nature of mind—is of fundamental importance for Buddhist traditions of meditation. But for many Christians, the recent explosion of new knowledge of the brain, in large part due to powerful new brain imaging techniques, has been perceived by many as a frontal attack on Christian tradition. Yet while Buddhists have been quite open to the work of the neurosciences, this openness has not been without tensions arising from the materialist metaphysics assumed by most scientists.

Here's why. The human brain is the most complicated biological structure that has evolved, at least as far as anyone at present knows. The reasons consciousness and cognition are so difficult to describe is that human beings have evolved the capacity for self-knowledge, meaning a certain access to ourselves that gives us subjective experience, which in turn gives us a way of looking at the world from where we are, as if we were on the inside looking out. This is extremely difficult to understand. Each of us is trapped inside our brain, and therefore within a particular point of view and time frame, with the capacity to reflect on that particular point of view and time frame. But we cannot get inside another person's brain, and no one else can get inside ours. So, the undeniable fact that we have particular perspectives is not closely paralleled with anything else we know about. The only thing we really know by experience in the whole universe is ourselves, but we are not sure about each other. This is the problem of other minds.

In thinking about mental and emotional experience, most contemporary neuroscientists assume that the mind is what the brain does in a biological and environmental context. The human brain is perhaps the most beautiful object that exists, at lease on this planet, because it allows us to perceive beauty, experience a self that in some sense is self-identical through time while we are alive, know something about the structure of existence, and have religious experiences like Awakening or union with Christ. But how does the matter of the brain, which weighs about three pounds and has the consistency of curdled milk, bring into existence our capacity for self-awareness and self-reflection? What is the brain's relation to the intellect, compassion, love, and hope or to more negative emotions like fear, anger, or hatred? How does a three-pound lump of meat connected to a central nervous system contextualized by environmental factors engender experiences like Awakening or union with Christ?

For twenty-five hundred years, Buddhists have employed strict training techniques to guide their mental states away from destructive emotions toward a more compassionate, happier frame of mind. Encouraged by thirty years of physical evidence of the brain's plasticity, neuroscientists are now taking a keen interest in how Buddhist meditation changes the mind/brain. Richard Davidson at the University of Wisconsin, Madison, has been studying the brain activity of Tibetan monks, in both meditative and non-meditative states. Using brain scans, Davidson had earlier demonstrated that people who are inclined to fall prey to negative emotions display a pattern of persistent activity in the right prefrontal cortex. When Davidson ran the experiment on a group of senior Tibetan monks skilled in meditation, the monks' baseline activity was much further to the left than previously demonstrated in anyone.[27]

A number of experiments monitoring brain waves using the electroencephalograms of individual Zen monks and nuns during sessions of meditation have been performed. Bain waves are a measure of the aggregate activities of large groups of neurons within areas of the brain that allow researchers to detect broad patterns of activity during specific kinds of activities. It was discovered that meditational states correspond to distinct brain-wave patterns and that the transitions into more advanced states of meditation can be correlated with further brain wave changes.[28] Each monk went through a series of four distinct stages during each meditation session, beginning with alpha waves, typical of both inward focused attention and deep relaxation, and ending for advanced meditators with theta waves, which are usually associated with drowsiness and hypnotic states. Only those monks who had meditated for more than twenty years showed theta activity. Also, the Zen master who guided the monks' practice could accurately distinguish between those monks in different states of meditation without resorting to brain-wave data.[29]

Of course, these experiments neither prove nor disprove Buddhist claims about Awakening, or that Awakening is reducible to brain states. I know of no Buddhist teacher who makes such a claim. But brain imaging research does suggest that the practice of meditation over time can lead to experiences that are, to some degree, quantifiable. In the case of Zen practice, prolonged meditation leads to distinctive patterns of brain activity, and these patterns probably correlate with specific kinds of experiences. One possible implication of this experimental result is that religious experiences produced by the practice

27. Reported in *National Geographic*, March 2006, 31.

28. Hood, Spolka, Hunsberger, and Gorsuch, *The Psychology of Religion*, 407ff.

29. Kasamatsu and Hiraim "An Electroencephalographic Study of Zen Meditation (*Zazen*)," summarized in Peterson, *Minding God*, 107.

of meditation are merely the result of cultural conditioning, as claimed by Stephen Katz.[30] If religious experiences like those produced by meditation or contemplative prayer are purely a cultural construct, the sort of physiological changes that are observed during prolonged periods of meditation or contemplative prayer should not matter. It appears to be the case, however, that cultural context over time produces new physiological states, which in turn lead to new cultural possibilities. That is, levels of human experience turn out to be biologically and culturally interdependent.

This is one reason that most Buddhists do not normally experience the neurosciences as a threat but as empirical evidence that supports the positive benefits of meditation. Many Buddhists claim, for example the Dalai Lama, that this same evidence empirically confirms the truth of the doctrines of impermanence, nonself, and dependent co-origination. Other Buddhists concur. David Galin, a psychiatrist associated with the Tibetan lineage of Buddhism, arrives at a similar conclusion, but from a different direction.[31] He argues that the "chaotic state" of Western scientific accounts of the human self, particularly those of the neurosciences, are inadequate from the standpoint of Buddhist practice and teaching. His argument is that the reductionist neuroscientific accounts of the biochemical foundations of mind are inadequate because they leave actual subjective experiences out of their accounts. While such "objective" accounts are accurate, they are incomplete. Buddhist practices of meditation, which focus on analyzing the subjective experiences and emotions the mind experiences, should be brought into objectivist scientific accounts of the mind in order to obtain a more accurate description of mental experiences.

B. Alan Wallace has taken Galin's views to their most coherent conclusions.[32] His theory of human consciousness is grounded in his understanding of contemporary quantum physics and his considerable expertise in Buddhist philosophy and meditation. His thesis is that mind and matter, subjects and objects, arise from a unitary dimension of reality that is more fundamental than these dualities. Specifically he argues for a "special theory of ontological relativity" that asserts that mental phenomena are conditioned by the physical processes of the brain, but do not emerge from these processes. To empirically test his theory he utilizes the Theravada Buddhist practice of *samatha*

30. Katz, "Language, Epistemology, and Mysticism."

31. David Galin, "The Concepts of 'Self,' 'Person,' and 'I' in Western Psychology and Buddhism."

32. See Wallace, *Hidden Dimensions*.

or "calming meditation," which is also practiced as a preliminary discipline in Tibetan Buddhism, the purpose of which is to create a "kind of telescope" to examine "the space of the mind," which he believes might have its own existence independently of the physical properties of the universe.[33]

Two interdependent lenses form the foundation of Wallace's "telescope" for "exploring the space of the mind." The first lens is contemporary physics, primarily quantum theory as interpreted by John Archibald Wheeler, Anton Zeilinger, and Michael Mensky, all three of whom conclude that the role of the observer is crucial to the laws of physics at both the quantum microcosmic and the macrocosmic levels of physical reality. Wallace relies on the work of these three physicists to argue for the possibility that states of consciousness may exist independently of matter, which in turn may provide a solution to the "hard problem" of neuroscience: how to explain the emergence of non-physical mental phenomena from the physical processes occurring in the brain.

Accordingly, as Wallace interprets quantum physics, energy may surge out of nowhere for a brief moment; the shorter the interval, the briefer the energy excursion. When electromagnetic waves pass through space, they produce oscillations at every possible frequency. When all these energy fluctuations are added up, the result is a background sea of light whose total energy is enormous. This is called the "zero-point field of empty space." The zero-point energy of this field is huge, even as it is the field's lowest possible energy state, and all other energy in space is over and above it. Since the zero-point field is everywhere, we are effectively linked to it, while the world of light we see is all the rest of the light beyond the zero-point field. Wallace argues that this field may not only be filled with zero-point energy, which can be *objectively* measured by physics, but also permeated by consciousness, which can be subjectively examined with techniques of meditation.

Wallace's second lens is his appropriation of the "two-truth" epistemology of the Indian Buddhist, Nagarjuna, and the metaphysics of Yogacara philosophy. As pragmatic truths about the physical world, scientific truths are secondary truths that in themselves shed little light on the nature of reality as a whole. Absolute Truth, however, is metaphysical and is named by Wallace, following Nagarjuna, "Emptying." Emptying is the Absolute Truth to which buddhas awaken through the practice of meditation, according to Nagarjuna's Madhyamika or "Middle Way" epistemology. Accordingly, Wallace concludes, we err if we expect the natural sciences as now constituted to solve issues of

33. Ibid., 36–37.

a metaphysical or religious nature, for scientific methods and the materialist assumptions of these methods were never designed to probe such questions. Furthermore, as secondary truths, the primary weakness of physics and the biological sciences—because scientific methods ignore the subjective mental processes of observers—is that neither discipline the mind nor give an adequate account of subjective mental experience.

On the other hand, Wallace argues that Tibetan Buddhist contemplatives have developed a highly specialized language to describe "the space of awareness" which he thinks is identified with the "substrate consciousness" (*ālaya-vijñana*) of Yogacara Buddhist philosophy. It is the substrate consciousness that Wallace identifies with the zero-point field of empty space. Buddhist texts characterized the substrate consciousness as bliss, luminosity, and non-conceptuality. Wallace claims that persons experiencing this mental state can "remain effortlessly in it for at least four hours—with physical senses fully withdrawn and mental awareness highly stable and alert."[34] While maintaining this state of awareness, the meditator observes that specific mental phenomena like desire, fear, aversion, hope, pain, and joy do not emerge from complex configurations of matter, as is widely assumed by the neurosciences, but rather from an underlying reality of archetypes "located" in the substrate consciousness. Practiced meditation places us in contact with these archetypes, which is the source of all mental and physical phenomena that the mind experiences.

So according to the "special theory of ontological relativity," all manifestations of mind *and* matter arise from a subtler dimension of "pure forms" or "archetypal symbols." At this point, Wallace argues, physics and Buddhist philosophy draw similar conclusions about the structure of existence: everything and every event is interdependent, observation conditions what is observed, neither space and nor time are absolute. But contemplative methods and scientific methods differ. Physicists and biologists rely on third-person observations and experiments that structure out subjective mental experience for consideration as empirical evidence is *quantitatively* analyzed. But Buddhist meditative methods rely on first-person observations and experiments on mental and physical phenomena in conjunction with *qualitative* analysis of experienced mental states. Accordingly, combining scientific third-person accounts of physical reality with Buddhist first-person analysis of mental phenomena would go far to resolving the "hard problem" of neuroscience: how to coherently explain the emergence of mind from physical processes.

34. Ibid., 45.

Exploring how the neurosciences might serve as a lens for understanding Christian contemplative experience and a number of Christian theological doctrines are central questions in the work of Eugene d'Aquili and Andrew Newberg, who have coined the term *neurotheology* as a description of their work. According to their theoretical approach, the mind functions through a filter of seven interdependent "cognitive operators," which are somewhat analogous to Immanuel Kant's categories, that act on the information the brain continually receives through the senses: (1) the holistic operator, (2) the reductionist operator, (3) the causal operator, (4) the abstractive operator, (5) the binary operator, (6) the quantitative operator, and (7) the emotional operator.[35]

The causal operator, for example, is responsible for seeking out causal relationships, and the reductionist operator analyzes an object or an idea in terms of its parts, while the contrasting holistic operator tries to perceive parts as parts of a larger whole, or gestalt. D'Aquili and Newberg locate these cognitive operators in specific areas of the brain, although the evidence for some of the cognitive operators, such as the emotional operator, which they identify with the limbic system, is better understood than others, such as the binary operator, which they do not assign to any location in the brain.

According to d'Aquili and Newberg, these seven operators give a complete account of the brain's cognitive functions, and thereby explain many forms of religious experience and symbolic expression. But their focus is on what Sells calls apophatic experience, or what they refer to as the "experience of absolute unitary being" (AUB), which occurs cross-culturally. Unlike Sells, they regard AUB as the primary form of religious experience, while Sell's work pays closer attention to forms of religious experience in which subject awareness does not disappear during mystical experience, referred to by scholars of mysticism as "cataphatic experience." d'Aquili and Newberg do not concern themselves with cataphatic experience to any significant degree.

The core element of d'Aquili and Newberg's theory that has attracted the most attention is their account of how AUB arises in the brain. Activities such as ritual and meditation work toward achieving various levels of AUB by causing a cascade of events that stimulate emotional pathways at the same time that areas in the prefrontal lobe of the cerebral cortex associated with special orientation are cut off in a process called "differentiation." Since the parietal lobe is involved in spatial awareness and self-other distinctions, blocking off these areas would, they claim, result in the emergence of AUB.

35. D'Aquili and Newberg, *The Mystical Mind*, 50–52.

Differentiation is said to occur as the result of overstimulation of the sympathetic and parasympathetic systems in the brain, which are, according to d'Aquili and Newberg, responsible for states of arousal and quiescence. Normally, they two systems compete with one another. However, religious activities, such as repetitive ritual dancing or focused meditation, often result in a kind of spillover effect that activates a conscious state of AUB.[36]

It is clear that d'Aquili and Newberg conclude that brain states are the primary causal agents of unitive experiences like AUB. It is this point, of course, that stimulates Buddhist interest in the neurosciences, since Awakening as a AUB experience is something that is pursued by an individual meditator's self-discipline and effort. But for Christian tradition and practice, the question of the causation of religious experiences is of greater importance since religious experiences like AUB are generally understood to have God as their source. In other words, Buddhist non-theism seems, at first glance, to fit more tightly with d'Aquili and Newberg's research than Christian theism. However, d'Aquili and Newberg have performed SPECT (Single Photon Emission Computed Tomography) scans on Franciscan nuns during prayer. Here, the SPECT showed differentiation in the parietal lobe, which they claimed confirmed that the nuns experienced a form of AUB during intense focused prayer.[37]

If such scans do in fact reveal the physical component of religious experiences like AUB, should we conclude that what shows up on the SPECT scans do not support the claim that God is the source of religious experiences in the minds of nuns at prayer? Are such experiences merely self-generated by the concentration and verbalization that is normally part of prayer? The scans of the nuns' brains indicated heightened activity in the forebrain and verbal association areas, but this is to be expected in any verbal task. Without a control group, it is not possible to know with any certainty whether this pattern is distinctive. Moreover, since prayer is most often not accompanied by AUB experience—a fact attested to by most Christians and Christian contemplatives—it remains unclear how the data gathered by d'Aquili and Newberg about Franciscan nuns at prayer should be interpreted.

Still, research such as d'Aquili and Newberg's raises important questions about how we should think about religious experiences in general and the unitive experience of Awakening in Buddhism or apophatic forms of Christian mystical experience in particular. The neurological foundations of

36. Ibid., 199–203.

37. Research cited in Peterson, *Minding God*, 113.

religious experience seem to engender a bit of a paradox for both Buddhists and Christians: as neurological research confirms the reality of religious experience, it simultaneously threatens to undermine Buddhist and Christian claims about its nature and cause. For example, would damage to the left parietal lobe affect a meditator's ability to achieve Awakening? Are such experiences truly cross-cultural, suggesting a potential unifying principle for the world's religions? If so, would this constitute a biological argument supporting the pluralist view I described in chapter 1 of this book? But is unitive religious experience reducible to the neurological functions of the brain? Is this really all there is to it?

Buddhist and Christian contemplatives assert that this isn't all there is to it. At this point, the most that can be said is that neuroscientific research on religious experience is still in its infancy, and perhaps a healthy agnosticism regarding the correlation of brain states with religious interpretations about the nature of the objects the brain experiences is for now the most viable position.

CONCLUSION IN PROCESS

Given the fact that neuroscientific research on meditative and contemplative experience is still in its infancy, conclusions must be tentative. The data is very limited, and much more research is required before any scientific account can be authoritative. Still, contemporary research in the neurosciences does in fact pose an important question about how contemplative experience should be understood and exactly how contemplative experience is manifested in the brain. The claim that contemplative experiences are *merely* a derivative of culture is inadequate because biochemical processes within the brain appear to play a causal role. Simultaneously, however, experiments within the neurosciences do not show that cultural elements are not part of contemplative experience, because achieving a meditational state of experience through rigorous practice requires significant preparation, training in specific techniques, and discipline of the intellect through doctrine—all aspects of culture. It remains true that religious persons experience what their particular traditions train them to expect to experience *even as* biochemical causal factors are at work in human brains.

So, while research like that of d'Aquili and Newberg's can offer coherent scientific accounts of the experiences and bliss that mystics in all religious traditions have reported, it does not support stronger religious claims about the origin and significance of these experiences wither in Buddhism or in Christianity. From a purely neuroscientific standpoint, there remains plenty of room to interpret AUB experience as either an experience of Awakening or the love of God. The question is always, what exactly do such experiences reveal about reality?

There appear to be at least two possible interpretations of the physical evidence gathered thus far. First, one could argue that the existence of brain states that correlate with AUB experiences demonstrates that these experiences do not point to anything objectively real other than the biochemical processes going on in the human brain. They are then essentially illusory states that are no different from states induced by drugs or brain damage. While scientific materialists most often draw this conclusion, d'Aquili and Newberg argue that the correlation of brain states with certain kinds of religious experience does not prove that these experiences do not have a referent outside the brain or that religious experiences are necessarily delusional, in spite of the fact that any experience can be delusional.

Second, this acknowledgement does not establish that religious experiences such as AUB connect us to a sacred reality existing independently of our experiences that is named differently by different religious traditions, but it is also false to conclude that they do not.[38] Certainly, it may well turn out that brain states are purely natural processes possessing no objective or supernatural component. Experience, including religious experience, does not interpret itself. What is needed, therefore, is a larger religious framework than religious traditions at present possess based on multiple considerations, in which biological, cultural, and historical considerations will play contributing roles. Such a framework will need to be metaphysically pluralist in structure in order to provide an account of these powerfully transformative experiences within the broader context, in this case, of Buddhist and Christian doctrine and practice. I have outlined a Whiteheadian pluralist viewpoint in chapter 1 which may provide fresh avenues for the practice of interreligious dialogue. If experiences like AUB turn out to be cross-culturally universal, which is the stance of students of mysticism like Michael Sells, and if they are understood to give genuine insight into the nature of reality—the way things really are— we might finally have a common foundation for interreligious dialogue.

38. One of several points argued by Barbour in "Neuroscience, Artificial Intelligence, and Human Nature."

6

Creative Transformation at the Boundaries

PROCESS AND PROCESS THOUGHT

The thesis running throughout this book is that interreligious dialogue is a process. It is clear from what I have written in chapter 1 that my understanding of the meaning of "process" is deeply informed by the philosophical and theological traditions that draw their primary inspiration from Alfred North Whitehead and Charles Hartshorne and known by such designations as "process thought," "process philosophy," and, if one is engaged in theological reflection, "process theology." It is also clear that the vision of theological pluralism I described in the same chapter is grounded in Whiteheads's metaphysical vision, including his vision of God, although I do not claim that all process thinkers would draw the same conclusions as I regarding the nature of religious pluralism. Indeed, most process theologians would not accept my reinterpretation of John Hick's "pluralist hypothesis," preferring a more inclusive theology of religions. The pluralism of viewpoints among process thinkers exemplifies the pluralism that Whitehead believed was deeply ingredient in the structures of existence itself.[1]

To argue that interreligious dialogue is a process—of which Buddhist-Christian dialogue is one example—requires clarification about the word "process." Although there is great diversity of opinion among process thinkers, most are rooted in Whitehead's *Science in the Modern World*, *Process and Reality*, and *Modes of Thought*. These writings reveal that Whitehead was not

---

1. For a good introduction to process philosophy and theology, see Cobb and Griffin, *Process Theology*; see chap. 1 of that volume for the basic concepts of process philosophy.

only a philosopher, but a mathematical physicist who believed that the dualistic and materialistic worldviews that still haunt Western culture generally, as well as much contemporary philosophy and current scientific opinion, are seriously misleading. Process thought affirms that process is fundamental, but it does not assert that *everything* is in process. Doing so would mean that even the fact that things and events are in process is subject to change. At this point process thought is in some disagreement with Buddhism's structuring worldview, which asserts that *everything* is in process. In Whitehead's thought there existed unchanging principles of process and abstract forms, which he called "eternal objects." But in his view, to be *actual*, that is, concrete, is to be in process. Here, of course, one can apprehend the influence of Plato on Whitehead's thought. Like Plato, Whitehead's point was that anything that is not a process is an abstraction, not a full-fledged actuality, which Whitehead called "actual entities" or "actual occasions of experience", as opposed to abstract forms that he referred to as "eternal objects."

More specifically, Whitehead proposed a metaphysics of organic events whereby the word "energy" is more helpful in understanding what is fundamental in the physical universe than "matter," so that process thinkers conclude that the units of energy (actual entities)—atoms, electrons, subatomic particles, of which all things ("societies of actual occasions") are constituted— are events rather than objects. Accordingly, rather than viewing the units of physical reality as tiny lumps of matter that act on one another only externally, Whitehead thought of these events as momentary happenings or energy events largely constituted by their internal and external relations with events in their past. They are interrelated occurrences of energy rather than self-contained material atoms, a view that is in consonance with contemporary quantum physics and relativity theory.

Whitehead viewed process as a temporal transition from actual entity or occasion of experience to another actual entity. These entities are momentary events which parish immediately upon coming into being. In Whitehead's language, they become "objectively immortal." Time in this view is not a single smooth flow, but comes into existence in incredibly small droplets of experience. A favorite analogy among process philosophers is a motion picture: the picture appears to be a continuous flow of images, whereas in reality it is constituted by a series of distinct photographic frames projected on a screen. The idea that true individuals are momentary bits of experience means that what we normally refer to as "individuals"—the sorts of things that endure through time like tables, books, chares, trees, rocks, rivers, our pets, our friends, religious human beings—are not true individuals but "societies" of individual occasions of experience. Personal human existence is a "serially ordered society" of actual occasions of experience over time.

Besides the process of transition from occasion to occasion that constitutes temporality, Whitehead wrote of another kind of process. The real individual occasions of which the temporal process is constituted are themselves processes of their own momentary becoming. From an external, temporal point of view, they appear to happen at once. Yet at a deeper level they are not "things" that endure through a tiny droplet of time unchanged, but are events taking a bit of time to become actual. Whitehead called this becoming "concrescence," which means, "becoming concrete." Here, the analogy of the motion picture breaks down because the individual pictures on the film are static, whereas the individual occasions of experience are dynamic acts of concrescence.

It is this dual emphasis on the process of transition and the process of concrescence that opens the way for understanding a large variety of religious experiences, including the processes of Buddhist-Christian conceptual, socially engaged, and interior dialogue. First, the process of transition establishes the importance of time. One occasion of experience succeeds another. The past is composed of those events that have occurred; the future is radically different, since it contains no occasions; and the present is the occasion that is now occurring in anticipation of future possibilities. The present is influenced by the past and it will influence the future when it becomes past. The "arrow of time" flows asymmetrically from the past through the present into anticipation of future possibilities. For process thought, there can be no denial of the reality of time nor can there be any notion that time is cyclical. Every moment is new and none can be repeated.

Second, the experience of an "eternal now" becomes intelligible. In the process of concrescence itself there is no time. This does not imply the existence of static entities because the successiveness of transition does not apply in the process of concrescence. Every particular moment of a fully concrete actual occasion is a "now," which in this sense means that it is timeless, or again in Whitehead's language, "objectively immortal." As objectively immortal, it becomes part of the past of which future occasions of experience must take account in their concrescence. In other words, the structures of existence are historical. The present is constituted by its "prehensions," meaning how it positively or negatively takes account of ("prehends") the past, which in turn engenders anticipation of future possibilities not yet fully realized, which when realized themselves become the past of which new future events must take account to become actual, *ad infinitum.* This is the structure of Whitehead's notion of "creative transformation."

Because of its historical character, the practice of Buddhist-Christian dialogue exemplifies the processes of creative transformation that is at the heart of nature. Entering into Buddhist-Christian dialogue means taking into account the past history of both Buddhist and Christian traditions. This includes their respective histories, classical doctrinal formulations understood in their historical contexts and how the meanings of classical teachings and practices have been adjusted to the conditions of contemporary experience; the ways in which culture influenced the development of Buddhist and Christian practice as both traditions spread from their original settings and encountered new traditions; the pre-modern, modern, and post-modern histories of Buddhist-Christian encounter; the effects of the natural sciences on contemporary Buddhism and Christianity. Thus being a contemporary Buddhist or Christian is a different experience than being a Buddhist ten, twenty, fifty, or hundreds of years ago even if the defining core of contemporary expressions of Buddhist and Christian self-understanding are defined in terms of classical teachings and practices.

The present is always in continuity with the past for contemporary Buddhists and Christians, but what the past presently means as Buddhists and Christians anticipate the future is different from what the past and the future meant to Buddhists and Christians living in the past. How contemporary Buddhists and Christians creatively encounter their respective histories will create future anticipations that are not yet fully actual, just as it did for Buddhists and Christians living in the past. If these future anticipations become actual in the future they immediately become part of the past of which new generations of Buddhists and Christians must take in account in relation to the future conditions of their existence that are unique to them.

Being a Buddhist in dialogue with Christian faith and practice creates a Buddhist self-identity that is different for Buddhists not engaged in dialogue with Christianity. Being a Christian, in my case, a Lutheran Christian, in dialogue with Buddhism (and the natural sciences), has created for me a different Christian self-understanding than I had before I entered into dialogue with Buddhism almost thirty years ago. Of course, one's self-identity is never a permanent achievement, but is also a process that one undergoes from birth until death. Furthermore, my particular experiences of creative transformation are not normative for other Buddhists and Christians. Still, I am not aware of any Buddhist or Christian who has engaged in conceptual, socially engaged, interior, or all three forms of dialogue, who has not been in some way creatively transformed.

Most often creative transformation through dialogue involves "passing over and returning" to one's own Buddhist or Christian tradition; most often one's self-identity remains Buddhist or Christian, but without the religious exclusivism that haunts most conventional Buddhist and Christian practice.[2] That is, one's Buddhist or Christian faith and practice is likely to assume an inclusivist character, with the theology of a minority of Christians assuming a pluralist character.[3] For other participants, the experience of creative transformation has led them to a duel religious identify as Buddhist *and* Christian. For example, Roger J. Corless, who died in 2007, identified himself as a Dominican oblate and a Tibetan Vajrayana Buddhist.[4] Still again, for others, like Rita M. Gross, creative transformation through dialogue with Buddhism has led her to leave her original Christian tradition altogether because her experiences within a particular denomination of Christianity were extremely dehumanizing. She is now a leader in Buddhist feminist scholarship and advocacy as well as a nationally recognized teacher of Vajrayana Buddhism.[5] As a Lutheran Christian pluralist, I believe that her departure from her original Wisconsin Synod Lutheran community into her particular Tibetan Buddhist lineage was an example of creative transformation.

CONSTRAINED BY BOUNDARIES

As a mirror of interreligious dialogue in general, the mutual creative transformation of Buddhist-Christian dialogue can only occur when Buddhists and Christians "know each other," to borrow a phrase from the Qur'an. I have tried to summarize the ways through which Buddhists and Christians have come to know one another in my discussions of conceptual, socially engaged, and interior dialogue. It is evident that the more Buddhists and Christians

2. According to John S. Dunne, dialogue normally takes place within in two polar movements: "passing over" and "returning" to the home of one's own religious standpoint, but now deepened and enriched by the "odyssey" of the encounter; see Dunne, *The Way of All the Earth*, preface and chap. 1.

3. See Ingram, "Interfaith Dialogue as a Source of Buddhist-Christian Creative Transformation."

4. See Corless, "The Mutual Fulfillment of Buddhism and Christianity in Coinherent Consciousness."

5. Gross, *Buddhism after Patriarchy*, 291–304; and Gross, "Meditation on Jesus."

dialogically know one another new questions rise to clarity in sometimes startling, but always interesting, ways. For this reason alone, the process of Buddhist-Christian dialogue can never attain a final end. It always remains an ongoing process. Still, present trends can be identified and future possibilities suggested. What follows is my own portrait of these possibilities.

A fundamentally important question energizing Buddhist-Christian dialogue and Buddhist-Christian dialogue with the natural sciences is, what is reality, the real, the way things really are? Buddhist-Christian conceptual dialogue and its dialogue with the natural sciences has an epistemological agenda that also informs socially engaged and interior dialogue. Merely reflecting on formalistic statements about how Christian faith and practice can be creatively transformed through the appropriation of insights from Buddhism, or how Buddhist traditions of social engagement have been positively influenced by Christian social justice traditions, or how Buddhist and Christian meditational disciplines engender similar experiences of reality named differently in each tradition, are important concerns. But focusing *only* on these concerns runs the risk of comparative triviality. Buddhist-Christian dialogue and its dialogue with the natural sciences should focus on fundamental epistemological issues that cut across Buddhism, Christianity, and the sciences. What are the boundary constraints of Buddhism, Christianity, and the sciences and how do Buddhism, Christianity, and the sciences explore the boundaries between the known and the unknown? How do they participate in the human quest for knowledge? What do they conceive as unknowable?[6]

A boundary question is a question raised by science, Buddhism, or Christianity that cannot be answered by science, Buddhism, or Christianity. Boundaries are also moveable, which means that the frontiers of knowledge are often pushed back in both science and religion. Still, the shifting boundaries of knowledge exist within larger fixed limits of human knowledge. In the natural sciences boundary questions arise because of (1) the intentional limit of scientific methods of investigation to extremely narrow bits of physical processes while ignoring wider bodies of experience, and (2) the resulting incompetence of scientific methods when applied to aesthetic, moral, and religious experience. Boundary questions in the natural sciences (and in Buddhism and Christianity) constitute methodological, conceptual, and experiential constraints. For example, standard Big Bang theory about the origin of the universe imposes a temporal boundary that constrains what scientists can know about the universe. Why is there a universe at all? How did the laws of

---

6. For a fuller treatment of these questions, see Ingram, "Constrained by Boundaries."

physics come into being so that the universe itself could become a universe that human beings can rationally understand, which Einstein thought was the greatest of mysteries? The standard response is that cosmologists can describe *how* the universe originated with a high degree of probability, but are ignorant, or at least agnostic, about *why* the universe exists and *why* human beings can understand its structures. Here boundary questions generated by the application of scientific methods in cosmology creates metaphysical questions cosmology is incapable of answering. Whenever this occurs, an opening is created for Buddhist-Christian dialogue with the natural sciences.

Reflecting from a Christian perspective, this is why physicist and theologian Thomas F. Torrance concludes that the sciences reveal a natural order that is both rational and contingent, whose laws and initial conditions were not necessary, so that the combination of contingency and intelligibility energizes a search for new and unexpected forms of rational order. Consequently, Torrance argues, boundary questions encountered in the sciences reveal a religious dimension. He concludes that "correlating the rational order discovered in the natural order with God goes far to account for the mysterious and baffling nature of the intelligibility ingredient in the universe, and explains the profound sense of religious awe it calls from us, and which, as Einstein insisted, is the mainspring of science."[7] Similarly, Catholic theologian David Tracy maintains that the intelligibility of the universe requires an ultimate rational ground, which is God.[8] Of course, Buddhists draw different conclusions expressive of Buddhism's non-theistic character—the mix of intelligibility and contingency in nature is just a fact to be accepted that requires no explanation in terms of origin. Here, we encounter a scientific boundary constraint that elicits two incommensurable religious responses.

However, boundary questions are not limited to the natural sciences. Religious questions incapable of complete solution through the application of theological or philosophical methods arise at the boundaries engendered by what Joseph Campbell referred to as "the universals of human experience," meaning experiences human beings undergo no matter what their cultural or religious context is, but which are nevertheless contextualized by specific religious and cultural contexts. For example, the universal experience of suffering raises the theodicy problem for classical for Christian theism. How can a loving, omnipotent creator of the universe permit unmerited suffering? Here the assertion of God's creative power and love creates a boundary question

7. Torrance, "God and the Contingent World," 347.

8. Tracy, *Blessed Rage for Order*.

Christian theology cannot resolve apart from rethinking the nature of God, as in process theology.[9]

Anxiety and confrontation with death, as well as experiences of beauty, joy, and the longing for justice and community, are other examples of the universals of human experience. Buddhists and Christians theoretically interpret these experiential universals according to their particular texts, doctrinal formulations, and practices. But just as with the natural sciences, all religious constructs are historically and culturally bounded. Which means that as in the natural sciences, they are also theory laden, so that neither Christian theological reflection nor Buddhist doctrinal reflection can legitimately claim complete or certain knowledge. What, exactly, is the nature of God? What, exactly, is Awakening? The standard Christian and Buddhist response is that God and Awakening are ultimately beyond human thought because both transcend anything human beings can imagine them to be, or not to be—hence an epistemological boundary.

In other words, authentic Buddhist and Christian faith is lived at conceptual and experiential boundaries. It is here that Christian theological reflection and Buddhist doctrinal reflection can be creatively transformed by dialogue with the neurosciences. When taken non-reductively, the neurosciences offer explanations of both patterns of religious thought and behavior in terms of the interactions between cognitive processes occurring in the brain contextualized by environmental factors. Neuroscientific explanations are also evidence for the adequacy and coherence of Christian theological pluralism, my particular version of which was described in chapter 1. This is so because neuroscientific accounts of religious experience and behavior inform us that just as culture does not hover above cognition, cognition is not somehow isolated from culture. Certain conditions of our social and physical environments are broadly similar in all human populations and throughout much of human history, and activate and tune cognition in similar ways cross-culturally. The similarities of teachings and experience that occur in humanity's religious traditions may be in part explained in terms of the activation and tuning of species-typical cognitive capacities by regular features of the environment. The considerable differences between humanity's religious traditions—the localized features peculiar to all religious traditions—is potentially explainable in the same way. By investigating the myriad, complex, and variable interactions among brain, mind, body, and environment, the neurosciences offer testable hypotheses concerning particular forms of beliefs

9. Cobb and Griffin, *Process Theology*, 118–24.

in God, non-theism, meditative practices, rituals, complex theologies, and doctrinal traditions across cultures and religious traditions.

Yet to conclude that the existence of boundaries impose constraints on scientific, Buddhist, and Christian knowledge claims by no means implies that significant and reliable knowledge is impossible in the sciences, or in Buddhism, or in Christianity. To conclude that scientists, Buddhists, and Christians cannot attain complete knowledge via scientific method, Buddhist philosophy and meditational practice, or Christian theological reflection and contemplative practice because of boundary constraints does not imply that the sciences have not amassed an incredible body of reliable knowledge about physical reality, or that Buddhists or Christians have not accumulated large bodies of reliable knowledge about the structures of human existence. For this reason alone, the boundary constraints confronting scientists, Buddhists, and Christians constitute a reliable foundation for a trilogue between the natural sciences, Buddhism, and Christianity. To this date such a trilogue has not occurred to any significant degree. But incorporating the natural sciences into the process of Buddhist-Christian dialogue in all three of its forms will unleash new directions of mutual creative transformation never before imagined by Buddhists and Christians in dialogue. It is "dialogue at the boundaries" that is the source of Buddhist-Christian mutual transformation, and, if the sciences are included as a third partner, the creative transformation of the sciences as well.

The main reason this is so is that boundaries point to that which is transcendent to what we can conceptually say and understand. This is, of course, the most important lesson we learn from the interior dialogue between Christian apophatic mystical experience and what our Buddhist brothers and sisters tell us about the experience of Awakening and the emptiness of all conceptual discourse about Awakening, even Buddhist discourse. As Tom Christenson, who teaches philosophy at Capital University, writes: "Some people suppose that talk about transcendence is talk about the super-natural. This is not the way I want to use the term. Something is transcendent if it goes beyond ourselves, for example, if it calls us or demands something from us, or lures us on to a new level of seeing, understanding, or being." Then Christian cites one of my favorite hymns in the Lutheran liturgical tradition that is based on the Twenty-third Psalm: "Shepherd me, O God, beyond my wants, beyond my fears, from death into life." It is easy to understand a prayer to fulfill my wants or to avoid my fears. But how can I pray to move beyond my wants and beyond my fears? This is transcendence, when something that does not spring from my own wants and fears captures me and stretches me beyond my wants and fears, perhaps even beyond my imagining. "Such an encounter can be an occasion of my growth, my conversion, my death, my rebirth, my arrival as a new person."[10]

A story can do this. Insights into the physical process at play in the universe can to this. Dialogically encountering another person can do this. Christian experience of God's presence through centering prayer can do this. Buddhist experience of Awakening can do this. Engaging in Buddhist-Christian conceptual, socially engaged, and interior dialogue can do this. Engaging in a Buddhist-Christian-science trilogue can do this. The experience of transcendence has multiple particular forms, but each throws us, sometimes kicking and screaming, out of the conventional limits of our knowledge and linguistic constructs, into boundary constraints that expand our experiences into new possibilities never previously imagined or encountered.

So about ultimate transcendence, as I have imagined it my version of theological pluralism, be this God or Emptiness, can anything really be dialogically said? In an important sense, the answer is "yes," because a great deal has been said and written by Buddhists and Christians. Indeed, this book is an attempt to contribute to what has been said and what may be said. But can things be said about ultimate transcendence clearly and unequivocally? The lesson of Buddhist-Christian interior dialogue is, "no." This is why as a Christian I have come to understand that conceptual, socially engaged, interior, and science-religion dialogue is the proper form of meaningful theological reflection for life in a culturally and religiously plural world that is always undergoing process. So should Buddhists and Christians remain conceptually silent? Perhaps the best answer is, probably more than we do. When Buddhists and Christians do engage in dialogical conversation, we should speak and write mindfully, as Buddhist and Christian meditative experience informs us, aware of the temptations involved in trying not to speak or in speaking too much. Again, following the instruction of Buddhist and Christian contemplatives, in speaking about things that reflect transcendence we need to speak and write in an intentionally impaired language by using words that cannot be uttered, in language with a deliberately warped grammar of unsaying, words that always carry a warning, as in the *Dao De Ching*: the words we speak or write are not final words.

10. Christenson, "The Oddest Word: Paradoxes of Theological Discourse," 179–80.

Bibliography

Abe, Masao, and John B. Cobb Jr. "Buddhist-Christian Dialogue: Past, Present, Future." *Buddhist-Christian Studies* 1 (1981) 13–30.

Abe, Masao, and Norman Wadell, translators. "Dogen's *Bendowa*." *Eastern Buddhist* 4 (May 1971) 124–57.

Augustine. *Confessions*. Oxford: Oxford Univerisity Press, 1991.

———. *On Christian Doctrine*. Translated by D. W. Roberts. Indianapolis: Bobbs-Merrill, 1958.

Ayala, Francisco J. *Evolutionary and Molecular Biology: Scientific Perspectives on Divine Action*. Vatican City: Vatican Observatory Publications and the Center for Theology and the Natural Sciences, 1998.

Bancroft, Ann. "Women in Buddhism." In *Women in the World's Religions, Past and Present*, edited by Ursula King, 81–104. New York: Paragon, 1987.

Barbour, Ian G. *Religion and Science: Historical and Contemporary Issues*. San Francisco: HarperSanFrancisco, 1997.

———. "Neuroscience, Artificial Intelligence, and Human Nature: Theological and Philosophical Reflections." In *Neuroscience and the Person: Scientific Perspectives on Divine Action*, edited by Robert John Russell, Nancy Murphy, Theo C. Meyering, and Russell A. Arbib, 249–80. Vatican City: Vatican Observatory Publications, 1999.

Barth, Karl. "The Revelation of God and the Absolutism of Religion." In *Church Dogmatics*, vol. I/2, sec. 17. Edinburgh: T. & T. Clark, 1956.

Béthune, Pierre-François de. "Prayer as Path." In *The Gethsemani Encounter*, edited by Donald W. Mitchell and James Wiseman, 82–88. New York: Continuum, 1998.

Borg, Marcus. *Meeting Jesus Again for the First Time*. San Francisco: HarperSanFrancisco, 1997.

Cabézon, José Ignacio. "Buddhism and Science: On the Nature of the Dialogue." In *Buddhism and Science: Breaking New Ground*, edited by B. Alan Wallace, 35–68. New York: Columbia University Press, 2003.

Callicott, J. Baird, and Roger T. Ames, editors. *Nature in Asian Traditions of Thought*. Albany: SUNY Press, 1989.

Chappell, David W. "Buddhist Interreligious Dialogue: To Build a Global Religious Community." In *The Sound of Liberating Truth Buddhist-Christian Dialogues in Honor of Frederick J. Streng*, edited by Sallie B. King and Paul O. Ingram, 3–35. 1999. Reprint, Eugene, OR: Wipf & Stock, 2006.

———. "Buddhist Responses to Religious Pluralism: What Are the Issues." *Buddhist Ethics and Modern Society*, edited by Charles Wei-hsen Fu and Sandra A Wawrytko, 355–70. New York: Greenwood, 1991.

Christenson, Tom. "The Oddest Word: Paradoxes of Theological Discourse." In *The Boundaries of Knowledge in Science, Buddhism, and Christianity*, edited by Paul D. Numrich, 164–83. Religion, Theology, and Natural Science 15. Göttingen: Vandenhoeck & Ruprecht, 2008.

Cobb, John B., Jr. *Beyond Dialogue: Toward the Mutual Transformation of Christianity and Buddhism*. 1982. Reprint, Eugene, OR: Wipf & Stock, 1998.

———. "Beyond Pluralism." In *Christian Uniqueness Reconsidered: The Myth of a Pluralistic Theology of Religions*, edited by Gaven D'Costa, 81–95. Maryknoll, NY: Orbis, 1990.

———. "Buddhist Emptiness and the Christian God." *Journal of the American Academy of Religion* 45 (1979) 86–90.

———. "Can a Buddhist Be a Christian, Too?" *Japanese Religions* 10 (December 1978) 1–20.

———. *Christ in a Pluralistic Age*. 1975. Reprint, Eugene, OR: Wipf & Stock, 1999.

———. *The Structure of Christian Existence*. Philadelphia: Westminster. 1972.

Cobb, John B., Jr., and Christopher Ives, editors. *The Emptying God: A Buddhist-Jewish-Christian Conversation*. Maryknoll, NY: Orbis, 1990.

Cobb, John B., Jr., and David Ray Griffin. *Process Theology: An Introductory Exposition*. Philadelphia: Westminster, 1976.

Cook, Francis. "The Jeweled Net of Indra." In *Nature in Asian Traditions of Thought*, edited by J. Baird Callicott and Roger T. Ames, 213–30. Albany: SUNY Press, 1989.

Corless, Roger J. "The Mutual Fulfillment of Buddhism and Christianity in Co-inherent Consciousness." In *Buddhist-Christian Dialogue: Essays in Mutual Transformation*, edited by Paul O. Ingram and Frederick J. Streng, 115–36. 1986. Reprint, Eugene, OR: Wipf & Stock, 2007.

Crossan, John Dominic. *The Dark Interval: Toward a Theology of Story*. Sonoma, CA: Polebridge, 1988.

———. *The Historical Jesus: The Life of a Mediterranean Peasant*. San Francisco: HarperSanFrancisco, 1991.

Cunningham, Lawrence S. *Thomas Merton and the Monastic Vision*. Grand Rapids: Eerdmans, 1999.

Daly, Herman E., and John B. Cobb Jr. *For the Common Good: Redirecting the Economy Toward Community, the Environment, and a Sustainable Future*. 2nd ed. Boston: Beacon, 1994.

D'Aquili, Eugene, and Andrew B. Newberg. *The Mystical Mind: Probing the Biology of Religious Experience*. Theology and the Sciences. Minneapolis: Fortress, 1999.

Dawkins, Richard. *The Blind Watchmaker*. New York: Norton, 1986.

D'Costa, Gavin, editor. *Christian Uniqueness Reconsidered: The Myth of a Pluralistic Theology of Religions*. Faith Meets Faith. Maryknoll, NY: Orbis, 1990.

De Martino, Richard J., translator. "Dialogue East and West: Paul Tillich and Hisamatsu Shin'ichi." *The Eastern Buddhist* 4 (October 1971) 39–107; 5 (October 1972) 108–28; and 6 (October 1973) 87–114.

de Silva, Lynn. T*he Problem of the Self in Buddhism and Christianity*. New York: Barnes & Noble, 1979.

Dreyfus, George. "Meditation as Ethical Activity." *Journal of Buddhist Ethics* 2 (1995) 28–54.

Dunne, John S. *The Way of All the Earth: Experiments in Truth and Religion*. South Bend: University of Notre Dame Press, 1978.

Eck, Diana L. *A New Religious America: How a "Christian Country" Has Now Become the World's Most Religiously Diverse Nation*. San Francisco: HarperSanFrancisco, 2001.

Elie, Paul. *The Life You Save May Be Your Own: An American Pilgrimage*. New York: Farrar, Straus and Giroux, 2003.

Fiorenza, Francis Schüssler. *Foundational Theology: Jesus and the Church*. New York: Crossroad, 1984.

Galin, "The Concepts of 'Self,' 'Person,' and 'I' in Western Psychology and Buddhism." In *Buddhism and Science*, edited by B. Alan Wallace, 107–42. New York: Columbia University Press, 2003.

Gilson, Etienne. *The Christian Philosophy of Saint Augustine*. Translated by L. E. M. Lynch. New York: Random House, 1960.

Gross, Rita M. *Buddhism after Patriarchy: A Feminist History, Analysis, and Reconstruction of Buddhism*. Albany: SUNY Press, 1993.

———. "Meditation on Jesus." In *Buddhists Talk about Jesus, Christians Talk about the Buddha*, edited by Rita M. Gross and Terry C. Muck, 32–51. New York: Continuum, 2000.

———, and Terry C. Muck, editors. *Buddhists Talk about Jesus, Christians Talk about the Buddha*. New York: Continuum, 2000.

Gustafson, James M. *Protest and Roman Catholic Ethics: Prospect for Rapprochement*. Chicago: University of Chicago Press, 1978.

Gutierrez, Gustavo. *A Theology of Liberation: History, Politics, and Salvation*. Translated by Sister Caridad Inda and John Eagleson. Maryknoll, NY: Orbis, 1973.

Guth, Alan, and Paul Steinhard. "The Inflationary Universe." *Scientific American* 250 (May 1984) 116–28.

Habito Ruben L. F. "The Resurrection of the Dead, and Life Everlasting: From a Futuristic to a Realized Christianity." In *The Sound of Liberating Truth: Buddhist-Christian Dialogues in Honor of Frederick J. Streng*, edited by Sallie B. King and Paul O. Ingram, 223–38. 1999. Reprint, Eugene, OR: Wipf & Stock, 2006.

———. *Healing Breath: Zen Spirituality for a Wounded Earth*. Ecology and Justice Series. Maryknoll, NY: Orbis, 1993.

Halliwell, Jonathan J. "Quantum Cosmology and the Creation of the Universe." In *Cosmology: Historical, Literary, Philosophical, Religious, and Scientific Perspectives*, 477–97. New York: Garland, 1993.

Haught, John F. *God after Darwin: A Theology of Evolution*. Boulder, CO: Westview, 2000.

Hawking, Stephen W. *A Brief History of Time: From the Big Bang to Black Holes*. New York: Bantam, 1988.

Hick, John. *God Has Many Names*. Philadelphia: Westminster, 1982.

———. *An Interpretation of Religion*. New Haven: Yale University Press, 1989.

———. "The Non-Absoluteness of Christianity." In *The Myth of Christian Uniqueness: Toward a Pluralist Theology of Religions*, edited by John Hick and Paul F. Knitter, 16–36. 1989. Reprint, Eugene, OR: Wipf & Stock, 2005.

Hollywood, Amy. *The Soul as Virgin Wife: Mechthild of Magdeburg, Marguerite Porete, and Meister Eckhart*. Studies in Spirituality and Theology 1. Notre Dame: University of Notre Dame Press, 1995.

———. "Suffering Transformed: Marguerite Porete, Meister Eckhart, and the Problem of Women's Spirituality." In *Meister Eckhart and the Beguine Mystics*, edited by Bernard McGinn, 87–113. New York: Continuum, 1997.

Honda, Mahaaki. "The Encounter of Christianity with the Buddhist Logic *Soku*: An Essay in Topological Theology." *Buddhist-Christian Dialogue: Mutual Renewal and Transformation*, edited by Paul O. Ingram and Frederick J. Streng, 217–30. 1986. Reprint, Eugene, OR: Wipf & Stock, 2007.

Hood, Ralph W., Jr., Bernard Spolka, Bruce Hunsberger, and Roger Gorsuch. *The Psychology of Religion: An Empirical Approach*. New York: Guilford, 1996.

Howell, Nancy R. "Beyond a Feminist Cosmology." In *Constructing a Relational Cosmology*, edited by Paul O. Ingram, 104–16. Princeton Theological Monograph Series 62. Eugene, OR: Pickwick, 2006

————. *A Feminist Cosmology: Ecology, Solidarity, and Metaphysics*. New York: Humanity Books, 2000.

Inada, Kenneth K. "Environmental Problems." In *Nature in Asian Traditions of Thought*, edited by J. Baird Callicott and Roger T. Ames, 231–46. Albany: SUNY Press, 1989.

Ingram, Paul O. *Buddhist-Christian Dialogue in an Age of Science*. Lanham, MD: Rowman & Littlefield, 2008.

————. "Constrained by Boundaries." In *The Boundaries of Knowledge in Science, Buddhism, and Christianity*, edited by Paul D. Numrich, 105–28. Göttingen: Vandenhoeck & Ruprecht, 2008.

————, editor. *Constructing a Relational Cosmology*. Princeton Theological Monograph Series 62. Eugene, OR: Pickwick, 2006.

————. "Interfaith Dialogue as a Source of Buddhist-Christian Creative Transformation." In *Buddhist-Christian Dialogue: Mutual Renewal and Transformation*, edited by Paul O. Ingram and Frederick J. Streng, 77–96. 1986. Reprint, Eugene, OR: Wipf & Stock, 2007.

————. *The Modern Buddhist-Christian Dialogue: Two Universalistic Religions in Transformation*. Studies in Comparative Religion 2. Lewiston, NY: Mellen, 1988.

————. "That We May Know Each Other." *Buddhist-Christian Studies* 24 (2004) 135–57.

————. *Wrestling with God*. Eugene, OR: Cascade Books, 2006.

————. *Wrestling with the Ox: A Theology of Religious Experience*. 1997. Reprint, Eugene, OR: Wipf & Stock, 2006.

————. "To John Cobb: Questions to Gladden the Atman in an Age of Pluralism." *JAAR* 45/2 Supplement (June 1977) L753–88.

————, and Frederick Streng, editors. *Buddhist-Christian Dialogue: Mutual Renewal and Creative Transformation*. 1986. Reprint, Eugene, OR: Wipf & Stock, 2007.

Ives, Christopher, editor. *Divine Emptiness and Historical Fullness: A Buddhist-Jewish-Christian Conversation with Masao Abe*. Valley Forge, PA: Trinity, 1995.

Johnston, Philip. *Silent Music: The Science of Meditation*. New York: Harper & Row, 1974.

Jordan, Robert. "Time and Contingency in St. Augustine." In *Augustine: A Collection of Critical Essays*, edited by R. A. Markus, 255–79. Garden City, NY: Anchor, 1972.

Kaluphana, David J. "Toward a Middle Path of Survival." In *Nature in Asian Traditions of Thought*, edited by J. Baird Callicott and Roger T. Ames, 247–58. Albany: SUNY Press, 1989.

Kasamatsu, M., and T. Hiraim. "An Electroencephalographic Study of Zen Meditation (*Zazen*)." In *Altered States of Consciousness: A Book of Readings*, edited by Charles T. Tart, 501–15. New York: Wiley, 1969.

Katz, Steven T. "Language, Epistemology, and Mysticism." In *Mysticism and Philosophical Analysis*, edited by Steven T. Katz, 93–103. New York: Oxford University Press, 2003.

Kaufman, Gordon D. "Religious Diversity, Historical Consciousness, and Christian Theology." In *The Myth of Christian Uniqueness: Toward a Pluralist Theology of Religions*, edited by John Hick and Paul F. Knitter, 3–15. 1989. Reprint, Eugene, OR: Wipf & Stock, 2005.

Keating, Thomas. *Invitation to Love: The Way of Christian Contemplation*. New York: Continuum, 1997.

Keenan, John P. *The Gospel of Mark: A Mahayana Reading*. Maryknoll, NY: Orbis, 1995.

———. *The Meaning of Christ: A Mahayana Christology*. Faith Meets Faith. Maryknoll, NY: Orbis, 1989.

———. "The Mind of Wisdom and Justice in the Letter of James." In *The Sound of Liberating Truth: Buddhist-Christian Dialogues in Honor of Frederick J. Streng*, edited by Sallie B. King and Paul O. Ingram, 186–99. 1999. Reprint, Eugene, OR: Wipf & Stock, 2006.

———. "Some Questions about the World." In *The Sound of Liberating Truth: Buddhist-Christian Dialogues in Honor of Frederick J. Streng*, edited by Sallie B. King and Paul O. Ingram, 181–85. 1999. Reprint, Eugene, OR: Wipf & Stock, 2006.

Keller, Catherine. "Walls, Women and Intimations of Interconnection." In *Women in the World's Religions, Past and Present*, edited by Ursula King, 232–50. New York: Paragon, 1987.

King, Sallie B. "Buddhism and Social Engagement." In *The Sound of Liberating Truth: Buddhist-Christian Dialogues in Honor of Frederick J. Streng*, edited by Sallie B. King and Paul O. Ingram, 159–80. 1999. Reprint, Eugene, OR: Wipf & Stock, 2006.

———, and Paul O. Ingram, editors. *The Sound of Liberating Truth: Buddhist-Christian Dialogues in Honor of Frederick J. Streng*. 1999. Reprint, Eugene, OR: Wipf & Stock, 2006.

King, Ursula, editor. *Women in the World's Religions, Past and Present*. New York: Paragon, 1987.

King, Winston L. *Buddhism and Christianity: Some Bridges of Understanding*. Philadelphia: Westminster, 1972.

———. "Interreligious Dialogue." In *The Sound of Liberating Truth: Buddhist-Christian Dialogues in Honor of Frederick J. Streng*, edited by Sallie B. King and Paul O. Ingram, 41–56. 1999. Reprint, Eugene, OR: Wipf & Stock, 2006.

Knitter, Paul F. Preface to *The Myth of Christian Uniqueness: Toward a Pluralist Theology of Religions*, edited by John Hick and Paul F. Knitter, ix–xii. 1989. Reprint, Eugene, OR: Wipf & Stock, 2005.

———. "Towards a Liberation Theology of Religions." *The Myth of Christian Uniqueness: Toward a Pluralist Theology of Religions*, edited by John Hick and Paul F. Knitter, 178–200. 1989. Reprint, Eugene, OR: Wipf & Stock, 2005.

Kraft, Kenneth. *Inner Peace, World Peace: Essays on Buddhism and Nonviolence*. Albany: SUNY Press, 1992.

Kuhn, Thomas. *The Structure of Scientific Revolutions*. Chicago: University of Chicago Press, 1970.

Küng, Hans. *Christianity and the World Religions*. Translated by Peter Heinegg. Garden City, NY: Doubleday, 1986.

———. *On Being a Christian*. Translated by Edward Quinn. Garden City, NY: Doubleday, 1976.

Lacy, Hugh. "Empiricism and Augustine's Problem about Time." In *Augustine: A Collection of Critical Essays*, edited by R. A. Markus, 280–308. Garden City, NY: Anchor, 1972.

Lakatos, Imre. "Falsification and the Methodology of Scientific Research Programs." In *The Criticism and Growth of Knowledge*, edited by Imre Lakatos and Alan Muscrave, 91–196. Cambridge: Cambridge University Press, 1970.

———. *Mathematics, Science, and Epistemology: Philosophical Papers*. Vol. 2. Cambridge: Cambridge University Press, 1979.

———, and Alan Muscrave, editors. *The Criticism and Growth of Knowledge*. Cambridge: Cambridge University Press, 1970.

Lichtmann, Matia. "Marguerite Porete and Meister Eckhart: *The Mirror of Simple Souls* Mirrored." In *Meister Eckhart and the Beguin Mystics*, edited by Bernard McGinn, 65–86. New York: Continuum, 1997.

Lonergan, Bernard J., SJ. *Method in Theology*. New York: Herder & Herder, 1972.

Mansfield, Victor. "Time in Madhyamika Buddhism and Modern Physics." *Pacific World* 11–12 (1995–96) 28–67.

Maraldo, John C. "The Hermeneutics of Practice in Dogen and Francis of Assisi." In *Buddhist-Christian Dialogue Essays in Mutual Renewal and Transformation*, edited by Paul O. Ingram and Frederick J. Streng, 53–73. 1986. Reprint, Eugene, OR: Wipf & Stock, 2007.

Matsunaga, Daigan, and Alicia Matsunaga. *Foundation of Japanese Buddhism*. 2 vols. Los Angeles: Buddhist Books International, 1974, 1976.

McFague, Sallie. *Models of God: Theology for an Ecological, Nuclear Age*. Philadelphia: Fortress, 1987.

McGinn, Bernard. *The Flowering of Mysticism: Men and Women in the New Mysticism (1200–1350)*. The Presence of God: A History of Western Christian Mysticism 3. New York: Crossroad, 1998.

———. *Foundations of Mysticism*. The Presence of God: A History of Western Christian Mysticism 1. New York: Continuum, 1992.

———, editor. *Meister Eckhart and the Beguine Mystics: Hadewijch of Brabant, Mechthild of Magdeburg, and Marguerite Porete*. New York: Continuum: 1994.

McNamara, Jo Ann. "The Rhetoric of Orthodoxy: Clerical Authority and Female Innovation in the Struggle with Heresy." In *Maps of Flesh and Light: The Religious Experience of Medieval Women Mystics*, edited by Ullrike Weithaus, 9–27. Syracuse, NY: Syracuse University Press, 1993.

Merton, Thomas. *The Asian Journals of Thomas Merton*. Edited by Naomi Burton et al. New York: New Directions, 1975.

———. "Marxism and Monastic Disciplines." In *The Asian Journals of Thomas Merton*, 332–42.

———. "Monastic Experience and East-West Dialogue." In *The Asian Journal of Thomas Merton*, 309–25.

———. *Mystics and Zen Masters*. New York: Dell, 1967.

Mitchell, Donald W. "God, Creation, and the Spiritual Life." In *The Gethsemani Encounter*, edited by Donald W. Mitchell and James Wiseman, 27–33. New York: Continuum, 1998.

————, and James A. Wiseman, editors. *The Gethsemani Encounter*. New York: Continuum, 1998.

Moltmann, Jürgen. *The Church and the Power of the Spirit: A Contribution to Messianic Ecclesiology*. Translated by Margaret Kohl. New York: Harper & Row, 1977.

Montaldo, Jonathan, editor. *Entering the Silence: Becoming a Monk & Writer*. The Journals of Thomas Merton 2, 1941–1952. San Francisco: HarperSanFrancisco, 1996.

Murphy, Nancey. "Another Look at Novel Facts." *Studies in History and Philosophy of Science* 20 (1989) 385–88.

————. *Theology in the Age of Scientific Reasoning*. Cornell Studies in the Philosophy of Religion. Ithaca, NY: Cornell University Press, 1990.

————, and George F. R. Ellis. *On the Moral Nature of the Universe*. Theology and the Sciences. Minneapolis: Fortress, 1996.

Nakamura, Hajime. *Gotama Buddha*. Los Angeles: Buddhist Books International, 1977.

Nhat Hanh, Thich. *Being Peace*. Edited by Arnold Kotler. Berkeley: Parallex, 1987.

Paley, William. *Natural Theology and Tracts*. New York: King, 1824.

Panikkar, Raimundo. "The Jordan, the Tiber, and the Ganges: Three Kairological Moments of Christic Self-consciousness." In *The Myth of Christian Uniqueness: Toward a Pluralistic Theology of Religions*, edited by John Hick and Paul F. Knitter, 89–116. 1989. Reprint, Eugene, OR: Wipf & Stock, 2005.

————. *The Silence of God, the Answer of the Buddha*. Translated by Robert R. Barr. Faith Meets Faith. Maryknoll, NY: Orbis, 1989.

Peacocke, Arthur. *Theology for a Scientific Age: Being and Becoming—Natural, Divine, and Human*. Theology and the Sciences. Minneapolis: Fortress, 1993.

Peters, Ted. *Science, Theology, and Ethics*. Ashgate Science and Religion Series. Burlington, VT: Ashgate, 2003.

Peterson, Gregory R. *Minding God: Theology and the Cognitive Sciences*. Theology and the Sciences. Minneapolis: Fortress, 1996.

Porete, Marguerite. *The Mirror of Simple Souls*. Translated by Ellen L. Babinsky. Classics of Western Spirituality. New York: Paulist, 1993.

Queen, Christopher S. "Introduction." In *Engaged Buddhism: Buddhist Liberation Movements in Asia*, edited by Christopher S. Queen and Sallie B. King, 1–44. Albany: SUNY Press, 1996.

————, and Sallie B. King, editors. *Engaged Buddhism: Buddhist Liberation Movements in Asia*. Albany: SUNY Press, 1996.

Rahner, Karl. *Theological Investigations*. Vol. 5. Baltimore: Helicon, 1966.

Rahula, Walpola. *What the Buddha Taught*. Rev. ed. New York: Grove, 1974.

Rawlings-Way, Olivia M. F. "Religious Interbeing: Buddhist Pluralism and Thich Nhat Hanh." PhD dissertation, University of Sidney, 2008.

Redmond, Geoffrey P. "Comparing Science and Buddhism." *Pacific World* 11–12 (1995–96) 101–14.

————. "Introduction." *Pacific World* 11–12 (1995–96) 2–3.

Ruether, Rosemary Radford. "Feminism and Jewish-Christian Dialogue." In *The Myth of Christian Uniqueness: Toward a Pluralist Theology of Religions*, edited by John Hick and Paul F. Knitter, 13–48. 1989. Reprint, Eugene, OR: Wipf & Stock, 2005.

————. *Sexism and God Talk: Toward a Feminist Theology*. Boston: Beacon, 1983.

Rorty, Richard. *Philosophy and the Mirror of Nature*. Princeton: Princeton University Press, 1979.

Samartha, Stanley J. "The Cross and the Rainbow: Christ in a Multireligious Culture." In *The Myth of Christian Uniqueness: Toward a Pluralist Theology of Religions*, edited by John Hick and Paul F. Knitter, 69–88. 1989. Reprint, Eugene, OR: Wipf & Stock, 2005.

Sells, Michael A. *Mystical Languages of Unsaying*. Chicago: University of Chicago Press, 1994.

———. "The Pseudo-Woman and the Meister: 'Unsaying' and Essentialism." In *Meister Eckhart and the Beguine Mystics*, edited by Bernard McGinn, 114–46. New York: Continuum, 1997.

Smith, Wilfred Cantwell. *Faith and Belief*. Princeton: Princeton University Press, 1979.

———. "Idolatry in Comparative Perspective." In *The Myth of Christian Uniqueness: Toward a Pluralist Theology of Religions*, edited by John Hick and Paul F. Knitter, 53–68. 1989. Reprint, Eugene, OR: Wipf & Stock, 2005.

———. *The Meaning and End of Religion: A New Approach to the Religious Traditions of Mankind*. 1963. Reprint, Minneapolis: Fortress, 1991.

Sponberg, Alan. "Green Buddhism and the Hierarchy of Compassion." In *Buddhism and Ecology*, edited by Mary Evelyn Tucker and Duncan Ryukan Williams, 131–55. Cambridge: Harvard University Press, 1997.

Stace, Walter T. *Mysticism and Philosophy*. Philadelphia: Lippencott, 1960.

Stannard, Russell. "Where in the World Is God?" *Research News and Opportunities in Science and Theology* 1 (October 2000) 4.

Stenmark, Mikael. *How to Relate Science and Religion: A Multidimensional Model*. Grand Rapids: Eerdmans, 2004.

Streng, Frederick J. *Emptiness: A Study in Religious Meaning*. Nashville: Abingdon, 1967.

Suchocki, Marjorie. "Religious Pluralism from a Feminist Perspective." In *The Myth of Christian Uniqueness: Toward a Pluralist Theology of Religions*, edited by John Hick and Paul F. Knitter, 149–61. 1989. Reprint, Eugene, OR: Wipf & Stock, 2005.

Swindler, Leonard. *A Bride to Buddhist-Christian Dialogue*. New York: Paulist, 1988.

Taniguchi, Shoyo. "Early Buddhist Ethics and Modern Science: Methodology of Two Disciplines." *Pacific Work* 11–12 (October 1995–1996) 35–62.

Teilhard de Chardin, Pierre. *The Phenomenon of Man*. Translated by Bernard Wall. New York: Harper, 1961.

Tenzin, Gyatso [His Holiness the XIV Dalai Lama]. "Foreword." In *The Gethsemani Encounter*, edited by Donald W. Mitchell and James A. Wiseman, ix–x. New York: Continuum, 1998.

———. "Harmony, Dialogue, and Meditation." In *The Gethsemani Encounter*, edited by Donald W. Mitchell and James A. Wiseman, 46–53. New York: Continuum, 1998.

———. *Kindness, Clarity, and Insight*. Translated by Jeffery Hopkins. Ithaca, NY: Snow Lion, 1984.

———. "Understanding and Transforming the Mind." In *Buddhism and Science: Breaking New Ground*, edited by B. Alan Wallace, 91–103. New York: Columbia University Press, 2003.

———. *The World of Tibetan Buddhism: An Overview of Its Philosophy and Practice*. Edited, translated, and annotated by Geshe Thupten Jinpa. Boston: Wisdom, 1995.

Tillich, Paul. *Christianity and the Encounter with the World's Religions*. New York: Columbia University Press, 1963.

———. *Dynamics of Faith*. New York: Harper, 1957.

———. *Systematic Theology*. Vol. 1. Chicago: University of Chicago Press, 1951.

Torrance, Thomas F. "God and the Contingent World." *Zygon* 14 (1979) 329–48.

Toynbee, Arnold. *An Historian's Approach to Religion.* New York: Oxford University Press, 1956.

Tracy, David. *Blessed Rage for Order: The New Pluralism in Theology.* New York: Seabury, 1975.

Tucker, Mary Evelyn, and Duncan Ryukan, editors. *Buddhism and Ecology.* Cambridge: Harvard University Press, 1997.

Yagi, Seiichi. "Buddhist-Christian Dialogue in Japan: Varieties of Immediate Experience." *Buddhist-Christian Studies* 14 (1994) 11–22.

———. "Paul and Shinran, Jesus and Zen: What Lies at the Ground of Human Existence?" In *Buddhist-Christian Dialogue: Mutual Renewal and Transformation,* edited by Paul O. Ingram and Frederick J. Streng, 197–215. 1986. Reprint, Eugene, OR: Wipf & Stock, 2007.

Yagi, Seiichi, and Leonard Swindler. *A Bridge to Buddhist-Christian Dialogue.* Translated by Leonard Swindler. New York: Paulist, 1988.

Waldron, William S. "Common Ground, Common Cause: Buddhism and Science on the Affliction of Society." In *Buddhism and Science: Breaking New Ground,* edited by B. Alan Wallace, 145–91. New York: Columbia University Press, 2003.

Wallace, B. Alan. *Choosing Reality: A Buddhist View of Physics and Mind.* Ithaca, NY: Snow Lion, 1996.

———. *Hidden Dimensions: The Unification of Physics and Pure Consciousness.* New York: Columbia University Press, 2007.

Weinberg, Steven. *The First Three Minutes: A Modern View of the Origin of the Universe.* 2nd ed. New York: Basic Books, 1993.

Welthaus, Ullrke, editor. *Maps of Flesh and Light: The Religious Experience of Medieval Women Mystics.* Syracuse, NY: Syracuse University Press, 1993.

Whitehead, Alfred North. *Adventures of Ideas.* New York: Free Press, 1967.

———. *Modes of Thought.* New York: Macmillan, 1938.

———. *Process and Reality: Corrected Edition.* Edited by David Ray Griffin and Donald W. Sherburne. New York: Free Press, 1978.

———. *Science and the Modern World.* New York: Macmillan, 1926.

Wilson, Patrick A. "The Anthropic Principle." In *Cosmology: Historical, Philosophical, Religious, and Scientific Perspectives,* edited by Norriss S. Hetherington, 505–14. New York: Garland, 1993.